THE SILENT

CHANGE

Compiled by Raymond J. Arruda

THE SILENT CHANGE

The Silent Change

Copyright © 2010 by Raymond Arruda

In the U.S. contact:

Raymond Arruda

Email: jrraydj@gmail.com

Website: musicshopdj.com

ISBN 10: 14637157064

ISBN 13: 978-1463715069

Printed in the United States of America

We all have tremendous gifts. Life allows us a path to access them…

TABLE OF CONTENTS

ACKNOWLEDGMENTS | v

PRELUDE | vi

INTRODUCTION | viii

Chapter 1 | How It All Started | 1

Chapter 2 | The Beginning | 12

Chapter 3 | Dark Side | 16

Chapter 4 | Trying To Fit In: Girls, Drugs, and 45's | 26

Chapter 5 | A Hard Lesson Learned | 46

Chapter 6 | A New Family | 58

Chapter 7 | Smoke Shop: Nightlife and the Music Business | 66

Chapter 8 | The Seed | 81

Chapter 9 | Turning A Corner | 97

Chapter 10 | The Show | 100

Chapter 11 | The Show Must Go On | 124

Chapter 12 | Word Started To Spread | 132

Chapter 13 | Curtain Came Down | 138

NOTES | 150

ACKNOWLEDGEMENTS

In memory of my best friend Michael McDevitt who taught me "The Show Must Go On. It's not a job to do for people. It's an honor."

I thank God for the precious gift of my family. They have endured a long road with me. Thanks to my wife for her patience and support, and special thanks to a young lady who gave voice, helped write, and bring this book to life--my daughter Toni. I love you.

PRELUDE

Music had the ability to keep groups of people separate. My show had the ability to bring them together. Up until the late 1970s there was a vast range of music styles in the world, with a following in each and every style. People kept to their own music styles, aiding in their isolation and keeping them separate and in a place to judge one another. Because of this, people stayed with their own kind, never branching out or needing to be a part of the whole. All efforts to bring people together failed. The music world needed to unite. There would never be one music style that could please everyone, but there was about to be a new show that could please anyone.

One of the most powerful musical impacts in the history of the world has taken place right before our eyes. An unprecedented, never-before-seen music show was created, bringing people together, and no one saw it coming. Breaking through racial barriers, music prejudice, ethnic prejudice, and most of all, the ever changing generation gap, this show brought people of all ages, family, friends, and nationalities together. It all began when a Providence native, Ray Arruda, a.k.a. Jr. Ray, came up with a show mixing all types of music; disco, oldies, country, big band, line dancing, rock 'n' roll, rock, pop, R&B, kids' music, and more. Everyone said it wouldn't work. Jr. Ray proved them wrong and helped pioneer one of the most valuable concepts of all time, a now multibillion-dollar business being used all over the world. Read this great story and know the secrets of the Silent Change.

INTRODUCTION

History has shown remarkable unity among people in times of change, and organized social movements have reflected this throughout our existence. But there are also those times when people come together unaware of their power and their intentions, out of their need to reunify their roots and establish common ground. One such time in history is the evolution of the wedding/banquet Disc Jockey. Before the late 1970s, disc jockeying at weddings didn't exist. Where it did exist — on the radio, at the clubs and on the party scene — it was a simple matter of playing one album after the other, with no thought to how the various music genres complimented each other or affected people. No one thought to mix the various artists in different music styles together in a continuous beat flow so that the audience had an array of music styles at their feet, ultimately exposing them to a world of culture and life they may have otherwise ignored. Prior to this, it had been unheard of to try. DJ's were convinced it couldn't be done. But then the early 1980s brought about a mass movement that affected the entire globe from hemisphere to hemisphere. It was a time in our history that marked the unifying of our primal human need for celebrating life without any boundaries, judgments, opinions, or prejudice. It laid the groundwork for people to rejoice and purge their spirit of life's burdens. Before the mid-1970s, decades passed where cultures remained separate due to the impositions enforced upon them. Class distinction, race, religion, ethnicity, age, and geographic location were among the barriers to integration. When the cultural phenomenon of wedding disc jockeying emerged, everything changed. Underneath people's wills, spirals of life force were engulfing the mind and inviting their spirits to rejoice in the mood, in the moment, and without preconceived negativism. Regardless of the barriers, chains, and absolute words of "no," people's innate instincts propelled them to a place of "yes," a place of love, of happiness, and of common understanding. It was a melting pot for the masses, allowing them to let down their guard, remove the masks, and simply have a good time. Unbeknownst to the world at large, no one saw this coming. Although the show had all the sound in the world, it was silent; it was a change happening beneath our feet. While its desire rang ever so loudly in everyone's gut, no one dared push the envelope, not in this arena or any other that challenged society. But ever so gently, so silently, the change emerged with a force unprecedented. It catapulted a life essence into our existence that no one could turn their backs on. Key elements for the change occurred when several components existed simultaneously. First was the emergence of the wedding disc jockey, which allowed people to hear their personal form of music in its original state through a set of records used on turntables, allowing for its intended form of palpable energy to be broadcast through a good sound-system. Prior to this, bands primarily covered each song. The delivery never fully gave the audience the original intended quality and power of the song like the pre-recorded versions did. The wedding disc jockey was also responsible for delivering multiple genres of pre-recorded music for various age groups while all under one umbrella of music. This allowed the listener to hear their own form of music in a setting they would have normally been unable to hear. The second component to the Silent Change was the quality sound system used, which gave the listener a true emotional connection to each song through clear vibrational and audible sound waves with good feedback, treble, bass and reverb. Third, was the arena of a captive audience, centered around a particular guest of honor, be it the wedding couple, the anniversary couple, the birthday guest, etc. People responded differently to direction from an MC in an atmosphere that focused on the guest of honor. They allowed their guards to drop more easily than if they were in a different setting. The relationship people had with the guest of honor put them in a position to be more agreeable to change and ultimately doing something they may have otherwise never done. Bringing us to the fourth component of the Silent Change was the presence of the MC/crowd host known as the disc jockey, the type of disc jockey who didn't just spin records and allow the music to do the work by itself, but rather the type of disc jockey who was a mastermind at working the crowd and directing/orchestrating every minute of the event with various tactical strategies intermingling the guests as well as getting everyone in the room to enjoy the celebration of the event. And the last component for this incredible formula of life at its best in the Silent Change, was the people's ability to drop their guard and remove their fears, take off their masks and let their hair down. All of these key ingredients were responsible for the Silent Change to occur. It was a change that was beyond necessary and was desperately needed by every class and race of people. It was a change that brought them all together. The Silent Change has since grown into a massive form of heart-stopping palpable energy, reminding people what we're all here for; the need for expression, acceptance, laughter, and love and to do it together as one, united not separate. It became the one place where freedom was a thing of the present, no longer a dream or a wish impossible to realize. In this book you will read how Jr. Ray's disc jockeying show became the number one requested form of entertainment. You will learn how it became the platform for people to hear their own music, how it helped bridge the gap of racism, and how it brought all kinds of people together. You will appreciate the incredible show-stopping DJ techniques used by one of the pioneers in the industry. You will understand the art form that delicately combines wildly different styles of music and how that brings people together. You will understand how the Silent Change is a time that marks one of the biggest musical signposts in the entertainment industry, one of the most important music changes of all time. An idea that brought people together has now become a multibillion-dollar industry, changing the course of the world and affecting how people interact with one another.

And you will learn the autobiographical history of the DJ who perfected the craft of disc jockeying and what gave him his finesse, remarkable reputation, stage presence and uncanny ability with people in the business. Jr. Ray used techniques like entertaining, directing, and the "emcee" effect to captivate his audiences. A born entertainer, he was a truly positive life force, whose sole purpose was to make people happy. This, coupled with the gift to entertain, improvise, and not take "no" for an answer, led to his remarkable contribution to music history.

Some entertainers may have been experimenting with similar ideas but this is how it happened in Providence. This is my story.

HOW IT ALL STARTED

I've been around music all my life. My dad played the banjo as a child and soon thereafter went on to singing and dance. In his mid-twenties, he retired the banjo to our hallway closet, where I often went to look at it in admiration. It meant everything to me.

Dad had a gift for singing and at a young age fell in love with music. He sang around our home each day, and at Christmas time we shared my fondest memory. Each year I couldn't wait for Christmas, especially because of our traditional Bing Crosby, Perry Como, and Burl Ives albums. Our whole family would gather around the Christmas tree and listen to the narration of "The Story of the First Christmas" by Perry Como. My mother would light a candle that sat on the center of our coffee table and dim the lights to give way for the twinkling glow of our tree. My dad sang along to each and every song while the rest of us hummed the parts

1

we knew. The sound of the needle on the record and the warm glow of Christmas were imprinted on my mind forever. I was destined for music; it was only a matter of time.

One day when I was a young boy, an old black man by the name of Tom Brown sat me down for a personal music history lesson. He was a local musician who had been around the block a time or two. He said that back in the beginning of the twentieth century, the most widely accepted form of music was spiritual/gospel music. Most of the folks in those days went to some sort of congregation to pray, and thus any music that complimented those ideas was widely accepted by the majority. Anything outside of that realm was frowned upon. The music he played was known as "music of the devil" and severely condemned. Known as Dixieland Jazz, the music combined rhythms of various instruments in the brass section, like the trumpet and trombone, along with clarinet and two other instruments, usually the guitar or banjo but also possibly the string bass, tuba, piano, or drums. The sound was characterized by one front-line instrument, usually the trumpet, playing the melody, and other instruments improvising around that melody. The result was a completely different sound than spiritual music, and the locals were aghast. Tom and his friends were ousted by the local townspeople and were forced to play their music deep in the woods, where they couldn't be heard. Music of that day and decades to follow all had such barriers; walls which inevitably had to be breached.

The big band sound in the late 1930s, '40s, and '50s drove a dozen or so musicians around town from one major city to another to perform in various arenas. It coupled men and women together in situations that were unheard of in those days. It was socially unacceptable for women to fraternize with men without damaging their reputations. However, the big band musicians would continue on their paths, dancing dances like The Charleston, The Lindy, The

Waltz, The Fox Trot, etc. The dances were a bit "touchy-feely" for the current day middle-class citizen, and the name "Fox Trot" was a little too racy for them, especially with their children mimicking the dance. Parents banned their children from listening to such music and refrained from it themselves.

The year 1955 brought about all kinds of upheaval and craze with the emergence of rock 'n' roll. Parents were up in arms with the new-found sound influencing their children. Elvis Presley, Frankie Lyman, Bill Haley and The Comets, Jerry Lee Lewis, Little Richard, and Ritchie Valens brought the era to a whole new level. The kids of the decade were on fire with the new up-tempo sound and current-day dances. Older forms of dance moves had become newer versions of themselves with more modern vibes and different names. They had now been transformed into something entirely different. There were different styles for different kids-The Lindy turned into the JitterBug, Line Dancing went from The Alley Cat and

THE SILENT CHANGE

Bump Hop to The Hully Gully and The Stroll. The dance styles and music genres became popular with the teenagers, who were breaking free from the mainstream conservative middle-class mold. And it didn't stop there.

To add to the hype and chaos of the new found sound, popular entertainers such as Elvis changed the entertainment platform by adding risqué hip thrusts to his moves. This completely offended parents in the worst way. Culture shock set in, and gasps and whispers were among the murmurs being heard across the sound waves. People were in absolute disbelief at the sight of such profanity being displayed by an entertainer. Children were banned from watching the sexual act and televisions were unable to broadcast his movements. Elvis was filmed from the waist up. His appearances on national television were pivotal events for America because of his controversial dance moves. Not only that, his music was influenced by black rhythm and blues as well as country —another slow

5

change for modern America: a white man singing music with black undertones. Juvenile delinquency and changing moral values were on the rise with the cultural momentum quickly moving forward. Music was changing, and people were seeing the negative effects it had on their children.

Slowly, people began to adjust to the new music; time ultimately pushed the walls down as the ever-loving teenagers-turned-adults were the new generation in charge. They were known as the Baby Boomers, born between 1946 and 1964. They were crazed with the mesmerizing movements and gyrations of the rock 'n' roll phenomenon. They were now accustomed to the new sound of music, especially when it sounded remotely close to that of the genius, Elvis. The 1960s was a decade that brought about a time of rebellion and counter-culture, where everything was questioned, and drug use and experimentation were ever so prominent. Soon enough, a variety of sounds, ranging from modern rock to soul to pop were on the scene. One of the newer sounds was a style of soul music with a distinct pop influence known as Motown. The music played an important role in the racial integration of popular music and was a descendant from earlier soul, gospel, and brass rhythms. It descended from the Civil Rights movement and allowed Black Pride to take precedence. Examples of its artists were The Temptations and Smokey Robinson. The decade of the '60s also introduced three other main kinds of pop music: East Coast Doo Wop, introducing The Supremes; R&B and Soul, showcasing Ray Charles, Sam Cooke, James Brown, and Aretha Franklin; and surf music, headlining groups like The Beach Boys. Also new to the scene was perhaps one of the biggest influences of that era, the British invasion of The Beatles. Mainly due to the Vietnam War and an increased popularity of the peace and love movement, folk music became widely listened to also. Artists like Bob Dylan, Peter, Paul and Mary, and many others were on the rise. The electric guitar known as the Les Paul emerged, the unveiling of Woodstock occurred, and lastly, the decade brought to us modern rock groups like The Doors, The Rolling Stones, The Who, and Jimi Hendrix. The new generation had the desperate need to express themselves in every sense of the word. The deaths of President John F. Kennedy, Martin Luther King, Jr., Robert Kennedy, Marilyn Monroe, Sam Cooke, Otis Redding, and Patsy Cline, along with the breakup of The Beatles were enough tragedy to make an era lose its mind. People suffered, and this suffering catapulted their need for expression to larger heights. Too many good people died and "freedom" was now something that people were on the rise to get.

With the breakup of The Beatles, the 1970s marked the beginning of a difficult era. The deaths of Elvis Presley, Jim Morrison of The Doors, Jimi Hendrix, Janis Joplin, Louis Armstrong, and Bing Crosby all occured in the '70s. The time was bleak. Radical ideas of the '60s were now widely accepted and drugs, sex, music, and freedom were the way of life. Feminism, space exploration, antiwar protests, the Civil Rights movement, and the hippie culture were prevalent in this decade. Hallucinogens like LSD, mescaline, and psilocybin, A.K.A-magic mushrooms were widely popular, supposedly revealing one's "true self" and allowing for further freedom. Any and all boundaries were pushed and questioned, and most lived freely in whatever way that meant to them. Rock 'n' roll had become lost within the tragedies of the era. Disco, rock, and many of its sub-genres like hard rock, soft rock, country rock, southern rock, progressive rock, new wave, power pop, blues rock, funk, punk, easy listening, pop, country, R&B, and hip hop (revealed at the end of decade) made up the music of the era. Artists such as Donna Summers, The Bee Gees, Bob Marley, Michael Jackson, Pink Floyd, Led Zeppelin, Elton John, Billy Joel, Bob Seger, Bruce Springsteen, Aerosmith, Fleetwood Mac, The Eagles, John Lennon, The Who, The Carpenters, Stevie Wonder, The Jackson

5, and Abba were pioneers of the time.

With a variety of musical styles and the need for freedom, the emergence of the wedding disc jockey became inevitable. The decade also reflected cultural movements in need of solidarity. Although the appearance of living freely seemed prevalent, fear was a constant for a lot of people affected by an era characterized by the rise of nuclear power, racial riots, and hate crimes. There was a need all over the world for people to oppose those fears that fueled their unwillingness to shed past generations' conventional belief systems. Completely by accident, Jr. Ray's disc jockey show allowed people to come together, to remove the seeds of hate, and to abandon preconceived notions about music. Through giving respect to the audience's music styles, allowing people to be who they truly were, and through a play-by-play direction, Ray allowed people to come together, bridging the gaps of prejudice, culture, religion, and generation, to become one. His music show was a silent delivery of unity in its finest role. He brought people together in a celebration of life. He forced black and white to commingle, exposing them to each other's heritage of music, and eventually led them onto the dance floor together. The integration of Jr. Ray's music show was a movement to say the least; a time when people could not have been further apart from one another yet, were brought together in ways they would have never imagined.

THE BEGINNING

Born June 7, 1953, in the heart of Providence, Rhode Island, I entered this world the youngest child of four. Interestingly enough, the order in which you are born directly dictates how you will respond to the external world. I, being the youngest, entered the world last, bracing myself against the constant fractures infringed upon me by my siblings. I was born into a world of teasing and taunting, just like every other child whose rank in the birth order is last. I quickly learned to seek approval and acceptance of others in order to feel loved. Thus, I navigated through the world, people-pleasing to find satisfaction and happiness. And when I found harmony in music and entertainment, I found the pinnacle platform for my people-pleasing tendencies.

As far back as I can remember, I felt I was a

good kid who always wanted to laugh and have a good time. I dreamed about being a somebody," even amidst the difficult journey I endured through my grade-school years. I was a terrible reader and had a hard time keeping up. I fell behind in the curriculum and found myself lost and confused about the simplest of language skills—nouns, verbs, adjectives, what were they? These and many other fairly basic questions stumped me. I gave up on the book stuff. I wanted to immerse myself in another area of school. I tried sports but quickly found I was not cut out for them. The combination of uncoordinated movements coupled with a lanky physique was a recipe for disaster, to say the least.

And then, at age seven, I had my first crash course lesson in singing solo in front of my peers. My second-grade teacher pulled me up in front of the class and insisted I serenade them with a tune or two. I never felt so good in my life. From there, I would advance to the auditorium then on to the Fox Point

Boys Club, a local community center established to keep kids off the street. Not long after joining the club, I became the lead singer of the Harmonica Band. We got really good at our craft and began touring locally. First, we started with performances at various Boys Clubs around the state. We then ventured into arenas like political functions, elementary schools, and recreational parks, and before long we found ourselves on local television shows like The Jay Kroll Show, The Good Morning Show, and Salty Brine's Shack. We were gaining popularity and soon became the talk of the town. Eventually, I joined the glee club as a soprano singer with pipes strong enough to lead the RI Boys' choir at the New York World's Fair.

At age eight, I distinctly remember performing for my dad at his part-time bartender's job. By day, his trade was a foundry worker, a job that demanded much physical labor in molten-metals, industrial machinery, and casts of all sorts. My father enjoyed his part-time work; it was here that we would do most of our bonding. I would regularly bring him lunch, and he'd anxiously await my arrival. He was so proud and would insist I sing for everyone. Each day a new friend appeared, and I would serenade them as well. The song was always the same, "When Irish Eyes Are Smiling" by John McCormack. I would sing my soul out, and boy was it something. The patrons would stop and look; I had the spotlight. They passed around a black tattered hat, and I would actually receive a tiny portion of their wallets. This was the beginning of an evolutional but difficult journey into the entertainment business.

THE DARK SIDE

My mom, Amelia Arruda, Amy for short, was the greatest mother of all time. She was a simple woman, who loved my siblings and me more than anything. She would have given us the clothes off her back to make sure our needs were met. She went without so we could have the little things we enjoyed. With what little we had, we spent our money frugally, carefully picking out the one item of treasure for the year. Most kids got presents at holidays; we got them about once a year, when we could afford them. A stay-at-home mother, my mom catered to our every need, making breakfast, lunch, and dinner; doing the ironing, cleaning, laundry, shopping, yard work, etc. You name it, she did it. She was also the neighborhood "nurse," so to speak. She tended ours and everyone else's wounds. If you fell and cut yourself, my mom would pick you up and patch up the problem. We took kids

16

home from school almost every day to see our mother. She got out the vintage First Aid kit and went to town, wrapping and gauzing and band-aiding whoever needed tending to. She was well liked in our neck of the woods, Fox Point. That's where she got her first part-time job, at the local Fox Point elementary school. She worked at the same school I attended. This arrangement had its pros and cons; believe me, when I was in trouble, she didn't have very far to go to reprimand me. She was good at the discipline — not too soft, but not ridiculously tough either. I loved her so much and still do.

My three siblings were somewhat active in my life, although the age gap between us kept us at arm's length. Florence, Flowie for short, is my oldest sister. She is six years older than me. A good girl, very spiritual and kind, devoted to her role as a good Christian; we didn't have much in common as children. At the time, I thought she was crazy for being so straight-laced, but as we've grown older, she's shown me the power of good and what steady morals will do for a person.

Alton, my brother, is second in line; he is five years older than I am. He was a great big brother — tough, a sports fanatic into hunting, fishing, and fast cars. He was my idol; everything he did amazed me. He could also be your basic jerk that all big brothers can be, picking on me, teasing me, etc. He got a big kick out of scaring me. However, looking back over my life, it might have been the very thing that kept me out of a lot of potential trouble.

And lastly, there was my sister Phyllis, also known as Phe Phe. She is two years older than me. She was my partner in crime and my protector. We had her, mischief #1 and me, mischief #2. We could write a book on some of the adventures we went on, they were so elaborate. Throughout all the crazy wild times we faced together, the one thing we took away from the escapades was that we both shared oversized hearts.

And boy, did we feel the impact of life in that lane. Hurting hits us harder, love feels much deeper, and life is overall one big dramatic tale to tell. But in the end, we worked out the kinks, using our strengths in a positive way and understanding and tending to our weaknesses.

I lived a pretty full life with my siblings, needless to say. I was looked after by at least one of them from day to day. On one particular occasion when I was eight, my brother Alton had been asked to walk me to and from the Boys Club. It was a routine responsibility he often had. Sometimes he would make pit stops before heading home from the Boys Club, an act my mother would never approve. These stops were at hangouts for dead-end kids from the streets. My brother liked to mingle with the rebels from time to time. He would often go to the Fox Point park, the dump, the black bridge known as the Jack Knife Bridge on the Providence River, snake town and on occasions, the train tracks. Alongside the train tracks were eight-foot trenches. On this particular day, inside one of the trenches was a teenage boy who looked to be in some kind of fog or daze. We headed down there to see if he was hurt. When we drew closer we noticed he was breathing in and out of a small plastic bag, holding a can of Zippo lighter fluid. I realized he was breathing in the vapor. He was acting drunk, and I became increasingly more curious about his behavior and the effect of this fluid. He was high. My brother grabbed me and hurried out of there — he knew this wasn't the place for us. We got home, and I recall the image replaying in my mind. I couldn't fight the insatiable urge to go back there. I schemed up a lie to tell my mother: I would be in the backyard playing hide-and-seek with neighbors, ensuring my mother's inability to find me should she need to. It was a plan to buy me time. I darted out the door and headed to the train tracks, urgently needing to feed my curiosity. I arrived at the site, my heart racing and my palms sweaty. I was approaching the brink of intense anxiety; I knew there could be a consequence for my decision to be here, and worst of all, inhale the vapor. I ran into the trench and halted in front of the mysterious material left behind on the ground. I thought for a brief second about turning around and going home, but curiosity got the best of me. I picked up the bag, brought it to my mouth, and inhaled the remaining vapor. I distinctly remember the smell, because the naphtha reminded me of when I filled my father's lighters. I began to feel lightheaded and dizzy. Loud muffled noises rang in my ears and I mistook the noises for a helicopter sound. I thought it was hovering above the railroad tracks, but when I looked, I was alone. What was happening to me? This was a physical sensation I'd never had before—and I liked it. An exciting rush had engulfed me. I felt powerful, carefree, and happy. This sensation and the wish to experience it again provoked the spark of my future drug habit, a habit that would haunt me for years to come. I now had a secret, one I would keep hidden from the rest.

My singing continued better than ever, especially with the newfound help of my friend in a bag. I would extract remaining naphtha from my father's can of lighter fluid on occasions when I needed a pick-me-up. No problem was too big or small to handle with my "cure all."

At age twelve I had become very involved with the Boys Club, and that gave me much attention and self-confidence as well. My parents received an invitation to attend the Boys Club Annual Awards Banquet. They were so proud to celebrate my talent and gift with the community. When the night arrived, we were filled with energy and excitement. I, in my maroon blazer given to me by the Boys Club for the harmonica band, quickly headed out the door to the bus station. We didn't have much money, so the idea of having fine clothes and an event to attend was a huge deal in our home. I felt like a million dollars in that blazer, especially because most of my clothes were hand-me-downs.

When we arrived, we walked in the banquet facility and everyone looked great! It felt so prestigious and I was honored to be there. We sat in our seats and the ceremony began. The president of the Boys Club took the podium. His speech conveyed a message of discovery. "In all areas of life new discoveries are made and special people with raw talent and amazing gifts come along. The Boys Club of America has created a new award for individuals with multiple achievements and the incredible ability and gift within these achievements. This particular person has been involved in ceramics, wood shop, swim team, chess team, finger pool, and singing. He is one of the finest representations of the Boys Club and a remarkable display of talent. He has showcased his ability in television and in many other forums, and we would like to recognize him for his outstanding achievements. Raymond Joseph Arruda, Boy of the Year, please come up and receive your well-deserved award." It was magnificent!! I looked at my mother and father; their smiles were warm and proud. I was filled with such happiness. As I walked up the steps to receive my award, the president announced they had a special surprise to add to the evening. "We want to offer you a fully paid scholarship to the Berklee College of Music on the condition your academic performance continues to be above a C average." Incredible. I was given the honor of a scholarship to one of the most prestigious music schools in the country. It was a night I'll never forget.

The next few days were filled with rewarding feelings of joy. Maybe I could be someone after all. However, slowly the voice crept back in, the inner voice filled with negativity and fear; the one that would repeat the same debilitating and crippling mantras over and over and over: "You're not good enough. You'll never be good enough. The award and scholarship were nothing more than smoke and mirrors." I slipped away, the words slowly unraveling the life and spirit inside me. I would find my father's can of lighter fluid in my fingertips all too often. It numbed the pain.

TRYING TO FIT IN: GIRLS, DRUGS, AND 45'S

I gravitated to an older crowd of friends, sniffing airplane glue, chasing girls, and drinking. At age thirteen, girls were my main focus. I quickly found they didn't like boys who followed the rules. It was pretty sad, because that's where I naturally fit, singing with my harmonica band and people-pleasing the authority figures in my life. The girls however, were more attracted to the bad boy, someone who was breaking the law. I accidentally found this out when I got drunk one afternoon with my friends and started playing tough. Instantly, the girls surrounded me.

Thus, by day, I was the good boy, displaying the image of a saint; by night, I was destructively curious and out to see what else I might get my hands into. I began steeling G.I.Q, known as Giant Imperial

Quart, which were large bottles of Narragansett beer from my father, and bringing them to the park. My hope was to gain popularity among the tough guys— that seemed to be what the girls liked.

I had never been much of a fighter. I always felt "less than" because of that nagging sabotaging inner voice that said I was a 'nobody'; weak and insecure. So I schemed up every plan I could to seem cool and fit in. I stole beer from my father and cigarettes from the local market just to keep up. This double life went on through my teenage years: the clean-cut soprano-singing kid at home and the bad boy from the tracks with my friends.

My singing was still gaining me accolades. I was accepted into the RI Boys Choir led by Mr. Thomas Hallen. It was the number one choir in the state, showcasing all of the best singers. We performed in a number of shows, including a performance at the Veterans Memorial Auditorium with the musical accompaniment of the RI Philharmonic Orchestra. The RI Philharmonic Orchestra is a prestigious and professional classical music company. They are the best in the state, and I was honored to be a part of something with them. It felt amazing to perform with such distinguished professionals. It felt like I was in a Disney production with all of the string and brass instruments.

We also performed at the New York World's Fair held in Queens in 1964. The New York World's Fair was the third major world's fair to be held in New York City. The fair is best remembered as a showcase of mid-20th century American culture and technology. Our show took place in the Kodak display sponsored by Disney. We performed songs from the Mary Poppins soundtrack on what seemed to be the largest stage ever built. It had an enormous concert sound system, one that was over the top and scaled for thousands to hear. This arena was like no other I'd ever experienced, and it felt like the crowd went on for miles. The highlight of the afternoon was my solo "Chim Chim Cheree." In that moment I was a star. It was one of the most magical days of my life.

That evening, when the day ended, I was raring to go to keep the party going. I searched anxiously for my airplane glue and lighter fluid. I had remembered them being full, but these episodes of getting high were beginning to take their toll. At last, I found them. They were near a baseboard, stuffed up underneath the bureau and sure enough, were empty. I frantically searched the house for something that would give me a pick-me-up. I came upon spot remover. In an instant, I snorted it. Anything I could shove into my body to numb the pain was the target. I began to feel woozy and my vision was blurred. I had those black spots occur, the kind that develop when your oxygen is low and you're about to pass out. I sat. I was in a daze for at least ten minutes.

I began to lose interest in the choir. On one

particular occasion, an incident occurred that cemented my decision to quit. My choir teacher, delivering some paperwork to another coworker, noticed my friend and me horsing around outside of class. He thought it appropriate to approach us and take our heads and smash them together, perhaps to deter us from playing around in school. Why and for what reason he chose to be physical, I don't know, but the incident had such an impact that I never went back to choir again. I didn't like being treated like that by anyone, especially a teacher in what was supposed to be a safe and respected environment-school.

I avoided telling my parents I quit the choir and hoped I could keep it from them for a while. Then, shortly after, a notice was sent to my house. The choir was singing again with the RI Philharmonic at the Veterans Memorial Auditorium, a performing arts theater in downtown Providence. My mother was so proud of my achievement that she saved every last cent she earned in order to take the entire family to the show. I was sick to my stomach. How was I going to break it to her that I had quit the choir and wouldn't be singing? I couldn't. I was too afraid of a beating and worse than that, of breaking my parents' hearts. I was stuck.

I proceeded with the lie in full force. The night arrived and my heart pounded with anxiety. I didn't know what to do, so I let the night play out and hoped for the best. We all got ready in our best attire; I in my choir outfit and maroon blazer, my dad in his fedora hat and blue striped suit, and my mom in her cream-colored wrap dress with matching shoes. At six thirty on the dot, it was time to head to the bus station and see the night through. Out the door we went, one second closer to my demise. Our bus arrived at the auditorium, my parents exited and walked toward the entrance door. I stayed quietly in the backseat. I didn't want to get up. It took everything I had when I was finally able to exit the bus. "What's my next move?" I thought to myself as I reached the last step.

I frantically searched for a way out, an excuse, a sickness, something. Then, in a God-loving miracle, I looked to the left and noticed a side entrance. Relief came over me. I quickly blurted out, "The choir enters through the side door. You guys go ahead, and I'll see you inside from the stage." They bought it. I waited for them to enter through the main entrance then headed straight to the side door. It was locked. Shit. I was in serious trouble now. I searched for another way to enter the building but there was nothing. I stood in front of the door, hopelessly shamed at what was happening. In the middle of winter, the coldest night in January, I had nowhere to go. I couldn't go inside.

I wasn't about to interrupt the show on top of everything else. With a deep breath in, I looked around and then walked over to a house with a lounge chair outside and sat, waiting for two and a half hours, scared and frostbitten. What was I going to do? It was now time to face the music.

Finally the event showed signs of its end when people began to trickle out of the auditorium. My stomach was in knots. The feeling of impending doom settled in my every cell. I saw my father's hat and long trench coat through the crowd of people. I quivered as I hesitantly walked over to them, my head low and bracing myself for the blow of a lifetime. My sister ran to me. Clenching my teeth, I took a deep breath in as she yelled "Ray, Ray, were you sixth in from the right in the second row or fourth from the left, third row?"

I sighed in utter amazement and shock. Fast on my feet and with the need to save my ass, I replied, "Second row, sixth from the right." She ran back to my parents, who were walking towards us and said, "I'm right, I told you sixth in from the right, second row. I knew it was him." I couldn't believe my ears. Was this really happening? My parents approached me with hugs and applause. They were so proud of our show and how good we sounded. I hugged them back, of course. I was now home free. So I thought.

THE SILENT CHANGE

It wasn't long after this that my parents received the news of my quitting the choir. One Sunday after church mass, my mother ran into a choir mom who asked her why I left the group. My mother had no idea what she was talking about and defended me saying, "He's been there, whatever do you mean?" The woman responded by saying that she personally attended weekly practice with her son and I hadn't been there in over four months. Embarrassed and hurt, my mother began to weep. She apologized to the woman, saying this was a big misunderstanding and that she needed to speak to me right away. She hurried to the bus stop and went straight home.

When I arrived home that afternoon from a day out fishing with my dad, my mother sat quietly at the kitchen table gesturing for me to come sit down with her. She looked me in the eye and asked "What happened?" I froze. I didn't have an answer. She saw the look of terror in my eyes. And I saw the hurt and disappointment in hers. She got up from the table and softly whispered into my ear, "Six months. You're grounded for six months. Go to your room." And with that, it was the end of it. Yup, I was grounded, although it lasted only about two months--they eventually got over it. No TV, no toys, no friends.

When I finally did get to see the light of day, I rushed right out to my friends and began using drugs again. Marijuana was the new drug of choice in my teens. This drew me closer to girls I had sought after, but not quite enough to get them to notice me. The girls I liked were attracted to the older, tough guys in our group. I needed a way to change that, and the night of the Sugar Berry Dance held at Crescent Park in Riverside was the answer to my prayers. I had on my black leather jacket and derby hat, which I kept hidden in my garage to be worn on special occasions. Inside the dance, guys lined the wall, waiting for the opportunity to score with a girl. I too scanned the room for any glimmer of hope that might come my way. I knew I didn't have much game when it came to the ladies, though, and I needed another strategy to gain their affections.

Out of the corner of my eye I saw pretty-boy Bruce Estrella strut past me, headed straight to the dance floor. I sharpened my focus and studied him. He had the crowd eating out of the palm of his hand. It took a moment to process the information I was witnessing, but I saw him glide his foot across the floor, sway his arm to the right, snap, and turn. All the girls swooned in his direction. He was doing some kind of R&B Smokey Robinson-type dance and commanding the stage.

Bruce's action revolutionized the entire world of courtship for me. I was blown away. I wasted no time and moved in with swift intent to get what I came for. The clap of my hands and the stomp of my feet caught the eyes of the people near me. Adrenaline filled my body with excitement. I rocked my head back and forth, swaying to the beat of the music. "This is my time," I thought to myself. And with that, I had my first encounter with the "laws of attraction." The girls drew closer to me and before I knew it, a few of them had their friends ask me for my number. I had finally learned how to be the center of attention and the life of the party.

I was on my way, ready to conquer the world. I had become friends with the local girls of the neighborhood. Brenda, Dawn, Diane, and my soon-to-be girlfriend Gail, were part of the clique I hung with. They and their boyfriends would get together and listen to music. When I joined them, I made certain to play the best albums I had in hopes to impress them with my collection and hopefully win the affections of Gail. I had a fairly large repertoire of records, some from my parents, my siblings, my aunts, my friends, and some were from my own archives.

One afternoon, at age fourteen, I decided to ponder my relationship with Gail and the strategies needed to make her my girl. I remembered my previous lesson on attraction, and I knew there was a method to this madness, one which had a formula. It was merely a matter of dissecting my thoughts until the answer lay before me. Pacing back and forth in my room, I stumbled across a portable turntable I had borrowed from my brother. In an instant, the equation flashed before my eyes. I would repeat the lesson I learned weeks earlier only this time, slightly varied. I would use the law of attraction as my advantage and the entertainment platform as my vehicle. My plan was to hold a party at my home. The record collection and turntable were the steering wheel for the night's success.

That same weekend, my parents went out one night and weren't expected back till late. My father had his 'guys night out' at the local bar he was employed at and my mother was out shopping with my aunt Mary, who lived upstairs from us. It was my very first party. I was fired up; there was a palpable distinctive energy in my home that night. On the one hand, I was ready for the battle of a lifetime; on the other, nervous tension ate away at my soul. Would I be able to pull this off? Would I get caught? I pushed the fears out of my mind and trudged forward. I had a lot to do to prepare.

I tidied up the house and got my list together for what I needed. I had a bottle of Bali High, Tango, and a couple of cases of Narragansett beer. Food was not an option, as all my money went to the alcohol for the evening. Luckily, I had a friend who was able to get the liquor for me through someone he knew with a fake ID. I gave him a couple of extra bucks for the alcohol run. Next, was the invites, making a list. I called up all the crew, the girls from the block and their boyfriends—Jimmy, Bobby, Norman and a few others. Everyone arrived at my home at about seven o'clock and I got right to business. I played a song, gathered up the ladies, and we danced. When the song was about to end I emceed the party, instructing the crowd to remain standing until I changed the record. Once the music changed we continued to dance. From time to time, one of the guys would make a small attempt to join the ladies and me on the dance floor, but when their courage failed, I was there to peel them from their chairs and keep the party going. I would eventually do this for all the guys, and by the end of the night we had quite the bash established. These weekend get-togethers went on successfully for a good eight to ten weeks.

That first evening, everyone was enjoying themselves and I had my eye on Gail. It was my time to strike and go for the kill. With the music as my wingman, I needed to shimmy on over and ask her out. Maybe this display of crowd orchestration would be enough to impress her. Sure enough, after some time of trying to win the attention of Gail, we finally got together.

Our relationship was incredibly

tumultuous. Arguments began with a soft whisper and eventually escalated into verbal assaults on one another. This led to frequent break-ups and her in the arms of another. These times were difficult to swallow, and my ego and pride were taking a beating. Thus, I too would have my share of rebounds. But in the end, Gail was the girl I wanted. While I waited for her, it was hell in the hallway. Music and partying were becoming my primary focus.

At age fifteen, I took an interest in the local dance show, Wing Ding, filmed nearby on Tuesday nights. It was the place to be if you could be so lucky to land a role. Special invitation was primarily the way one would be asked aboard, however my friends and I devised a plan to get in against the odds. We would often visit the set on Tuesday nights in hopes to get a glimpse of the action. Crew members would frequently enter and exit the building while we sat on the sidewalk admiring the hustle. We felt if we were near their energy, maybe we'd get lucky somehow. One night, a crew manager approached the exit doors and yelled "Regulars." A line of people followed him in the studio, and in an instant, we had our chance. We came back the following week ready to sneak in. It was risky--we didn't know if they'd catch on. With our finest clothes and hair just right, we stood in a line. When the crew manager opened the door, game faces were on. "Regulars," he yelled, and off we went. We marched with an anxious confidence and prayed we'd get into the studio. We did.

Here we were, in the studio, in awe of our luck. Silently high-fiving each other and smiling with delight, we basked in the glamour of the evening. We were soon approached by the director and told to dance as well as we could. We took our cue and went to work. We danced a full hour. Our dance numbers ranged from The Skate, The Shing a Ling, The Funky Broadway, The Jerk, The Detroit, and The Fox Point Cha Cha to an assortment of freestyle moves. We were on fire.

When the night came to a close, I was so proud of having witnessed the close proximity of success's door and how I might integrate that into my life. It was the turning point for my recognizing I too could be a 'somebody'. Success was knocking and my dreams were awaiting their discovery. I packed up my arsenal of 45's — different from the kind Dirty Harry used — and began chiseling out my road ahead creating a dream I'd never imagined.

Spinning records at the Friday night get-togethers was vastly improving. My record-changing skills were flowing far better now than they had been. I developed a method of emceeing that allowed me to keep everyone dancing while I changed the music swiftly and without long pauses. I had begun brainstorming ideas of how I might turn this into something financially lucrative. I had a list of contacts who might help point me in the right direction and a notebook's worth of ideas. My intentions were to lay down a disc jockeying foundation that paid the bills, but I soon became sidetracked with a few hiccups in the road preventing my further production.

One Friday evening at our regular get-together at my house, a domino effect of events occurred, leading to police sirens, training school, and nothing short of an eye-opening experience. It spiraled into a life-altering scenario changing everything for me and proving to be a hard lesson learned, yet simultaneously enhancing the very core success I was searching for in the DJ business.

A guy by the name of Jimmie P. came to the house that night. He wasn't part of the normal Friday night crew and crashed the party uninvited. He was my brother's age and was known for being the tough guy of the neighborhood. He was a matter-of-fact type of guy, a real risk-taker. That night, he guzzled a pint of sherry wine in two seconds flat, unnerving everyone and raising the hair on our arms. We didn't question him or dare attempt to ask him to leave. He had a bottle of pills in his hand and was trying to sell them. Before he could make his rounds and get them sold, I heard my mother's voice saying her good-byes to Aunt Mary as she came to the door. Quickly we scrambled to clean up the mess and head out the back door. As my mother was turning the key, the last of my friends were jumping over the back fence. I noticed cans of beer lying against the couch. I ran over to conceal them before my mom came in, and I noticed the bottle of pills underneath the rocking chair. "Shit," I thought. The pills must have fallen from Jimmy's jacket as he ran out of the house. I reached under the chair and stuffed them in my pocket.

Smiling inside, I knew I was okay by the skin of my teeth. My mother entered the house with all her shopping bags and I grinned from ear to ear, like the perfect choirboy she knew I was.

A HARD LESSON LEARNED

The next night I headed to my good friend Norman's house. He had ties with Jimmy, and I needed to get Jimmy's pills back to him. As I walked up Norman's front lawn, I saw red flashing lights approaching. I hurried into the house to warn my friends, and noticed the scent of airplane glue in the air. I yelled "five-o," a popular warning that meant the police were coming, adapted from the popular TV show Hawaii Five-O. My friends, sniffing glue at the kitchen table, quickly hatched a plan. They would lock the front door and escape through the back. I would be knocking on the front door as if I had just arrived, and I could delay the police there.

We implemented our plan, and an officer joined me at the front door and walked with me into the house. He picked up the scent in the air and radioed for help. I tried to make small talk with him. His name was Suggarew. I recognized him as one of the neighborhood cops. He was scary and quite intimidating. When the backup cop came in the hallway, I was sure I would walk out of there with no problems. But to my surprise, the backup officer was the sergeant, the crankiest of all of the cops. He had a chip on his shoulder the size of Alaska. He eyed me up and down then asked me why I was there. Suggarew replied I had just arrived. He looked at him then back at me, "Book him," he said, and that was it. I was arrested. They searched me after putting cuffs on my wrists. I was in near shock that it went down like this. And of course, there they were, the pills. I frantically blurted out, "They're my nerve pills." They laughed at me, brought me to the squad car, then took me to the police station. My mother and father were called. I was charged with possession. Being a minor, I was released to the custody of my parents, landed a two-week punishment, and again my parents were very disappointed in me.

THE SILENT CHANGE

The night I got out of the house, I met up with a few of my older friends, Joe, Bruce, and Tony. We were joy-riding in Bruce's car when all of a sudden red flashing lights were behind us. "Not again," I thought. I was fairly confident I was in no real trouble, as I had done absolutely nothing wrong this time around, merely a case of bad timing. The police pulled us over and searched the car. In the trunk, they found a stolen tire. How they knew that I'll never know. We were all sent to the station and booked.

The owner of the tire dropped the charges and we were all relieved to say the least. I was ready to go when the officer told me I was to remain there until my parents were called. Apparently, the owner of the tire dropped the charges with the adult section of the police station but never made it to the juvenile end on the third floor of the building. I was still being charged with this offense. My parents arrived and were fuming. They had their words with me and I was punished for what seemed to feel like forever.

Thinking the past was behind me, I set my sights on new adventures to plan. But two weeks later, I walked to the front hall table to retrieve my notepad when I saw a summons envelope in the mail with my name on the front. Confusion overcame me. I opened the letter. It stated I was to appear in family court for two criminal charges: one, possession of barbiturates; and two, larceny of a tire.

My heart sank. I was innocent. Why was this happening? "Well, I'll go to court and explain my case. They'll give me a slap on the wrist and everything will be all right." The upside to all this mess was that I was gaining notoriety with my circle of friends. It gave me the "bad boy" status I was looking for, and ultimately I was better respected. My parents however, flipped their lids. They were pissed. My punishment was extended somewhere into the thirty-day figure. It was hard to keep track of the days, though, as my mind was going numb.

THE SILENT CHANGE

The court date soon arrived. My parents and I took our seats in front of the judge as he read the charges aloud. I explained my innocence in the matter and assured him of the confusion and mix up. The judge listened to my plea and continued reading my file. Then he looked up and stared directly at me. "What's this school offense about?" he asked. He read out loud how I had had a friend's mom sign a paper four months ago, saying we were moving away, so that I could drop out of school without my parents knowing about it. I stumbled over my words and looked in my parents' direction. My mother was devastated. The judge was disgusted. It was the nail that sealed the coffin shut. I was sentenced to F.O.C, better known as Further Order of the Court. I was incarcerated and sentenced to the Rhode Island boys' training school indefinitely. My mother began hysterically crying. I started to tremble and shake. The guards handcuffed me and brought me to a cell. The heavy iron-barred doors made a loud bang when they sealed me in. I was panic-stricken.

My father came in to say good-bye. He was a man who hardly welled up, let alone shed a tear, yet his eyes had filled with tears. Down his cheek the tear ran, and saddened words muttered from his mouth, "I tried everything I could, and now you must do it on your own." The guards escorted him out of my cell and back to the main hall. It would be some time before I would see my parents again.

I was placed in handcuffs and foot shackles. I boarded the prison van headed to the local training school. As I was transported to the facility, everything felt surreal. I was becoming increasingly numb and scared. The only sense of comfort I had was that the guards were pretty cool. I made certain I didn't give them a reason to be anything but cool towards me. Long before I got to the facility, I knew I had gotten myself into more than I could handle. Once there, I felt the long uncomfortable stares of the other inmates. I settled into my room, where I was locked behind a solid wooden door with cinder block walls attached to it. I peered out a small six-by-eight-inch window and wondered how I was going to get through this. Tears welled up in my eyes as I sat with feelings of utter loneliness and doom.

I tried to remain on my best behavior and lessen any sentence I had. I was placed in a cottage that housed a total of twenty boys. We became a family unit in a short time, a span of about three or four weeks. They educated me with some interesting "tools," if you will. I learned how to cheat at cards, how to hotwire a car, how to steal a car, how to sell stolen goods, how to deal with barbed-wire fences, and what to use and buy to get high. These were some of the life-changing tools that lined my road ahead.

Other interesting aspects to the training school were the various ethnicities that existed and how we got along. About three-quarters of our cottage's residents were black and the rest were a mix of white and Hispanic. But within these walls, color made no difference. We were all brothers. We had to be. It was us against the outside world. There was a lot of racial tension happening on the news in those days. Racism was still running wild and aggressive. We found it all utterly unnecessary. In fact, because of my black brothers, I have a terrific repertoire of Motown music in my collection and a performance style I use in my D.J. shows. My black friends were big fans of Smokey Robinson, Marvin Gay, Martha Reeves and The Vandellas, and James Brown. They had a handful of 45's and grooved to them with ease and flare. One particular guy, called Cline, was the star performer. He was a very talented dancer and entertainer. He was smooth, and would showcase a little routine to Smokey Robinson's "Baby Baby Don't Cry." As he danced, he would lip sing and gesture to the song. He would wave his finger in the no-no sign then bring his finger to his cheek just under his eye and wiggle it downward to signify not crying. I practiced these moves and began to master the art of miming the lyrics to a song.

Thank God for those guys. Not long after, Cline got released and left me his 45's. I've used them regularly and till this day, refer back to them when I'm on a show.

A week after I was incarcerated, a mass riot broke out in the training school auditorium. The inmates revolted against the staff members and broke and smashed whatever they could find. Staff members were beaten and eventually the riot moved outdoors. Cars, buses, vans, etc. were tipped over, smashed, and kicked in. It was pandemonium. State police were called in from Rhode Island, Connecticut, and Massachusetts. They surrounded the building from fifty yards away, lining the edge of the freeway. They had shields, blue helmets, and three-foot-long nightsticks. Marching into the rioting crowd with megaphones in hand, they were advising all inmates to get to the ground, hands behind them. Anyone who was not following these orders was severely beaten. The riot was soon under control, but a lockdown order was in effect for two weeks. All inmates were restricted to their cells and all privileges were taken away.

After a year at the RI boys' training school, I was up for a disciplinary review. An assessment was in order to check my progress within the facility. The review came and went. It seemed my behavior had gone from good to bad, and they were keeping me there until further notice. But I didn't care. I no longer cared about getting out of there. My interest in the real world was fading, and I was losing interest in life as well. Apathy set in and I was giving up.

A good example of this occurred when I had the duty of escorting a new inmate to his cottage. He was a just a boy, probably ten or eleven years old. He began mouthing off to me. I turned him around and whacked him in the back of the head. For an instant, I felt remorse but immediately after, my feelings numbed and I didn't care. I continued walking on in the direction of the cottage. When I got to the door, the kid I had hit entered before me. Suddenly, someone came from behind the door and kicked me, square in the abdomen, knocking me out. When I awoke, I felt dazed, confused, and disorientated. I stumbled back to my cottage and found it very difficult to breathe. I began to throw up blood and was rushed to the emergency room. I later learned I had a ruptured pancreas and was hemorrhaging from the abdominal area. I was successfully operated on and was placed in the ICU to recover. Later that afternoon, a visitor arrived at the hospital and informed me that my assailant was the cottage master, a correctional officer who was on duty at one of the cottages. He was an ex-marine with a second-degree black belt in martial arts. He was in charge of the cottage I was at earlier that day with the young boy. Apparently, he saw me hit him, didn't care for what he saw, and attacked me. That was hard to hear. It was a bit of a reality check.

My dad was called. He arrived at the hospital in no time and was grateful I was alive. He didn't approve of my overall attitude in the recent months and was sure I had something to do with being attacked. His feeling was I probably caused it. He was asked if we wanted to file charges against the man who attacked me and his reply was no. He felt it was my punishment for being in the training school in the first place. I was a little hurt and disappointed.

On another note, the parole board released me. They felt the discharge was necessary so that I could adequately heal and keep distance from my attacker. For the first time I began to feel again. I saw a glimmer of hope and desperately needed to plug in. I said my good-byes to my fellow inmates and headed off. This was the beginning to something, I hoped.

A NEW FAMILY

I reconnected with the crew from back home. I was now one of the bad boys, with a well-respected reputation. It was no longer difficult to get the attention of the girls. Gail took a liking to me again. We rekindled our relationship and set off for a happy romantic time together. It didn't quite work out as planned. I was not equipped, let alone prepared, for the turbulence before me. My people-pleasing and co-dependent tendencies allowed me to manipulate my way into a relationship that should have been over before it started. I was now set on a path that led me to a life of swollen pride, guilt, shame, and a lot of "less than feelings" that inevitably and recklessly came to an end.

Gail and I had been dating a couple of months when a bad situation got worse and we broke up.

THE SILENT CHANGE

I never wanted to see her again. I hoped this nightmare would go away. One night, lying in my bed, I heard a car approach. The door opened and shut, and there was a slight knock at the door. I opened the door, it was Gail. I was ready to shut the door when she stopped and asked me to hear her out, she needed a minute of my time. She apologized to me. I didn't want to listen any longer, but she forced the door open and blurted out the words, "I'm pregnant." I couldn't speak. I was in a place I'd never been before, at a depth never felt before, and at a place never more clear before this moment. I would have to deny all reason, all rational thought, and choose a road of hope, a road of life. Maybe, just maybe, there would be a new beginning.

I was sixteen years old, and Gail assured me I was the father. I believed her. I chose to stay and work things out. I chose to follow love for my unborn son's sake. I didn't know what would come from our relationship, but I knew I needed to give it a chance.

Gail deserved a partner, and my child deserved a father. I felt I had made many bad choices in the past. I needed to right the wrongs once and for all. I went to my father and told him of the situation and that I would marry Gail. He shook his head and said, "I knew you both were getting too close." He then said he respected my decision to marry her.

Gail and I could barely afford the hall for the wedding, let alone the music and food. We had rented a small banquet facility in Providence called the Brightridge Avenue Hall. It was minimally decorated and set with a lavender theme. Gail picked out the decor. She and her sister Dawn spent countless hours arranging centerpieces and decorating. Overall, everything was beautiful. We had a pretty-good-sized wedding party, with ten people, including Gail and me. We had a three-piece band; a singer, guitarist, and drummer. They were all right, but overall I wasn't happy with the music. I wanted something better. Our cake was purchased from a small shop nearby and

THE SILENT CHANGE

Gail's dress had been on sale at one of the wedding shops in the city. I looked handsome as could be in my light gray double-breasted suit. Gail looked stunning as well, especially with her baby bump. Our son would soon be born.

It was quite rewarding to see the important people in my life together, harmoniously sharing joy and happiness. Gail was a part of my family now and I kneeded to do my part. I said my vows to her and inside shivered with doubt. I knew we'd somehow do the work but how successful we could be was another story.

The day was nice. We had a beautiful ceremony and a great reception. We danced all night, regardless of the band's quality which was not that good, and when it was time to wrap up, we headed to my father's house to continue the party.

When I arrived at my father's house, I headed straight for my stereo and my 45's. As soon as the music started to play, the party exploded with excitement. I directed everyone to dance in the dining room and the parlor, and then with a speaker in the window, directed them to the yard outside. With an abundance of liquor and a night full of testosterone, the party was over the top. The best man and two of the ushers had words with a few half-drunk neighbors, and before they could be corralled, fists were swinging. The police were called and the three guys from my wedding party were handcuffed and arrested. Soon everyone headed home and Gail and I were left alone together, at last.

The old crew seldom got together anymore. Most of us had gotten hitched and were spending countless hours working to support our new families. I now had a job working at Bryant College as a cook. Gail had a career in jewelry. Before long she would leave work to give birth to our baby. I worked a typical forty-hour week, but it wasn't enough to support our way of life. We were saving to buy a home and had a little one on the way. When there was overtime, I lunged at it. I did what I could to support us, and the stress was getting more and more difficult to bear. At night, I often got high or drunk to feel good. Then, in my altered state of mind, the harsh realities from the past brought up many harbored pains and failed letdowns. I held on to this and many other betrayals to fuel my self-pity and give life to my resentments. Distrust resided in both Gail and me. I was accused of having affairs on many occasions and Gail gave me the third degree when I came home from a night out. Anger, rage, and paranoia filled my toxic state of mind. I used the nightclubs as a way to de-stress. My time in them, coupled with the addictions, were becoming a recipe for disaster.

The Birth: Raymond Joseph Arruda, Jr. was born in 1971. I was just about eighteen years old when I realized he was the breath of life I had been desperate to find. Everything that mattered was in this precious soul I was holding. To be a father was a miracle, a journey of unending love and commitment. I was incredibly blessed to have this path before me. Four children later, I still feel the same way about each one of them: Raymond, Jennifer, Donnie, and Toni. I often say to each of them, "You are the greatest gift God has given to me. Your children, my grandchildren, are living proof that life keeps getting better. I love you all."

Ray was sharp as a tack. He began walking at nine months and talking at ten months. He was very confident and smart beyond his years. Mentally, he was advanced about five or six years ahead of his contemporaries. He was well spoken, kindhearted, and keenly aware of his environment. He was the star of our first Polaroid camera. Jennifer, our second child, was born in 1972 . She was "Daddy's little girl." She was super-friendly and loveable and had the heart of a saint. She took dance lessons and always admired my performance qualities. Donnie, our third child, arrived in 1975 and was a whole new personality. He was mischievous and a daredevil. The risk-taker in our family, this boy was very adventurous. His cute little scheming smile would well up his eyes when he laughed and he had a heart of gold. Toni, our last child, was born in 1978. She was very outgoing. At a young age, she marched to the beat of her own drum. Her passion was to sing and dance. She used to perform Olivia Newton John's "Let get Physical" at four years of age. Life was good, and it seemed like maybe it could turn around for Gail and me.

SMOKE SHOP:

NIGHTLIFE AND

THE MUSIC BUSINESS

My wife and I would frequently go to nightclubs on weekends. When we weren't together, I would accompany the guys out on Friday nights. One Friday night, I bumped into an old friend from the neighborhood, Jimmy Ferris, who was currently writing music for a band he was starting. He asked me if I still sang and if I'd be interested in looking at some plans he drew up for his band. He showed me his notepad full of music, his guitar, and lastly, mentioned the key players he would ask for the formation of his band. He wanted a soulful jazzy sound similar to that of Tower of Power. We swung by his house, where he demonstrated the type of music he envisioned. There he had an Ampeg amplifier, a Fender telecaster guitar, and a black flat-top microphone with reverb. He asked me to join in his jam session. It felt amazing. I could picture myself live on stage delivering music to large crowds. We didn't waste time. Immediately I said yes to this venture. Our band was made up of Gary Jordan (drums), Wayne Manning (bass), Jimmy Ferris (guitar), and me as the lead singer. We called ourselves Smoke Shop. Wow, my dreams were finally coming true.

The band had to work hard getting people to our shows. We started out playing in the Fox Point Sportsman Club. We would call any and everyone we knew weeks before the gig to invite them. We then phoned everyone again the night before the show. Our marketing was of huge priority to us. It's what eventually put the bread and butter on our tables. A good friend of mine, Ernie Chaplin, my right-hand man also known as my partner in crime, helped me put flyers up all over town. We wanted to be somebody and did just about anything to make it work. Kevin

THE SILENT CHANGE

Crowshaw, our sound and light man, designed our first light show from old light outlets and switches that Ernie and I had taken from an abandoned house in downtown Providence. It was amazing to see what he did with what little he had. From time to time, we updated our collection with more creative ideas. Late one night Ernie climbed on the roof of the Providence aquarium and unscrewed an assortment of colored floodlights. They soon became the stars of our light show. Being a bunch of poor broke guys, we tried to measure up to the competition. We did whatever we could to have a complete show, even if it meant using unconventional methods.

One evening when we performed at the Sports Club, everyone applauded and commented on how professional and great we sounded and looked, especially our newest addition, the light show. Our band rehearsed for a short time at Jimmy Ferris's house, but after a fight broke out, we decided to research new places for rehearsal. We decided on the basement at my house. This would be a terrific place to rehearse the band, I thought. We began knocking down walls to have ample room for our set up. We used our martial arts inspiration, drawn from Bruce Lee movies, and began kicking down the walls. This ultimately ended up being our rehearsal space for the next seven years.

Soon personality conflicts ensued and Jimmy left the band. The new players were Gene Washington as guitarist, Larry Walker as alto saxophone player, and Dave Butler as horn player. I shared the front with added lead singer Greg Nutter.

We grew like any other newly formed band would. We had arguments, debates, brainstorms, and agreements. We eventually found our collective niches together and played a variety of shows with an assortment of crowds. We played the Knights of Columbus, the American Legion Post, the Masons, the Shriners, the Daughters of Ices, the Ramada Inn, the

Marriott, the Biltmore, Bristol Motor Lodge, sports clubs, weddings, showers, anniversaries, and birthdays. Each and every gig was a learning experience.

One night in December of 1978, we played a club in Connecticut. The show was well received and everyone had a good time. The night was winding down when I headed to the back office to collect our pay. I met with the owners and began squaring away our payment arrangement when one of them abruptly asked, "What are you doing with these black guys? Why are you running around with them?" I cleared my throat and shuddered at the thought of answering the question. I knew my response would get us thrown out and moreover, we'd get stiffed our money. The other owner asked me if I'd take a proposition of his: I would take a larger cut of money for myself in return for a smaller total on the bill. In short, the owners were asking me to screw my band members for a break on the cost of the show. At that moment, I felt ashamed to be white. The racism was beginning to cut through my skin more sharply than ever before. I was beginning to understand the barrier my brothers faced all these years. I looked the owner square in the eye and replied "No, thank you. There will be no deal today or any other day." They put the money on the table and asked me to leave. I took our earnings and left. Racism was still at large. Many people felt the edge of that blade and for most, the blade stuck for life. We were a family of brothers and took on each other's pain. I never told the other band members what went down that night; I didn't want to hurt them. On many other occasions, we faced the blade of racism. Until one night, we united as one. It was spring, in 1978, when we played a show at the IBA club in Providence. Something extraordinary had been brewing in the air, awaiting the right moment to unveil itself. Tonight was that night. Unbeknownst to us, we were in for quite a ride.

The evening began on shaky ground. I had learned we would play my first show to an entirely black crowd. I quivered at the thought of how this would play out. Would we get booed off the stage because the front man of the group was white? I had a massive pit in my chest, giving me a bit of anxious tension. I felt I wasn't able to embody soul, a key ingredient for performing to a black crowd. I wasn't the same color as my brothers, and in my opinion, I felt soul came from the depths and ancestry of many years of suffering. It was their beautiful gift, bestowed upon them for all they endured. I felt I had no business either pretending to have soul or performing with my brothers in this situation. But I didn't have a choice. I was prepared to get up on stage and do the best I could with what rhythm and voice I had.

I took to the stage and began setting up our equipment, my heart racing. I took out the microphone and began prepping for audio quality. "Check one, check two, check one, ch ch check." As I talked into the mike, a black guy walked up to me, got really close to my face, and directly over the microphone asked,

"What color are you, boy?" The reverb and the clarity of his voice rang through the crowd. I froze in horror. I looked out in the sea of people and saw eyes intensely staring me down, awaiting my answer. This was one of the most intimidating moments in my life, I couldn't move. Smitty, the drummer, yelled, "Don't listen to 'em—we're not here to satisfy his ego."

I listened to Smitty and disregarded the man in my face, shuffling for something else to do till he exited off the stage. It was time to begin our set. We started with a few easy jazz groove songs. The timbre in the bass began the melody, and off we were with the first song. The crowd observed our every move and slowly took us in, beginning to sway their heads to the beat. It was about all we could muster out of them, and we were spent when it finally became time for our break. I went behind the stage, quiet and withdrawn. I felt alone and lost out there on stage, completely out of my element. The two horn players, Larry and Dave snickered at my solemn behavior. I noticed they were

73

directing their laughter at me and I blurted out, "What's your problem?" They stared me down and continued to laugh. This is cruel, I thought. I was being called out by the crowd, and now my band mates are ganging up on me too. Larry responded with "You ain't shit out there tonight, Jr."

"What's your problem?" I asked. "I'll tell you your problem. You're the nigger tonight. You're the minority. Get used to it. What you're feeling, we deal with every day from white people. Since I moved here from New York, I get the stares and glares every time I enter the supermarket, every time I go to work, and every time I'm somewhere my color doesn't fit in. I get the feeling of judgment and discomfort from people's gestures, comments, and sometimes direct name-calling. Now you're feeling it. But there is one difference tonight: we're with you. We know you better; we know who you are, and what you're all about. Since the day I first met you, you've always made sure everyone was feeling okay. In your home, at rehearsals, you offer beverages and food. You call us and ask our input, you treat us like your family. And mostly, you're not racist. I know you got what it takes to make it. Those people out there work hard all week, and they're out there tonight to have a great time. They're no different from any crowd we've played for—white, ethnic, mixed or whatever. Just get that crap out of your head. You can give them what they want. We wouldn't be here if you didn't have what it takes. You're good at your job, Raymond. Don't let that negative shit take you out. Go on out there and do what you do."

I was silent. Struck by the nerve that was plucked and strung, I awoke. I would fight, damn it, Thank GOD for Larry, he brought me face to face with a fear that had laid deep inside of me for a long time. Secretly that voice would tell me over and over I wasn't good enough. My peers and my brother Larry were telling me I was good enough. Larry suggested a prayer, GOD help us to overcome our difficulties and bring us together as one. Amen.

The next set was to begin any moment. The impatient crowd was ready for an evening of excitement. No one in the audience had been sold on our first set, and no one had given themselves permission to let loose. This set would be critical in the success of the evening. It was SHOW TIME.

"And now ladies and gentlemen, a performance of unparalleled proportions, of unseen dimensions and indescribable capabilities, by two of New England's hardest-working showmen in the business. Let's give a warm round of applause for Greg and Ray." The crowd was stunned, in awe of our stylized introduction given by our Monty Hall Vegas style impersonator, our horn player, Dave Butler. No one was expecting what we gave them, and everyone wanted more. Greg and I ignited the stage with an entrance complete with a choreographed routine, costumes, and lighting. Having had a costume change, he and I wore bright yellow seventies-style bell bottom jump suits with zippers at the ankle, deep-blue-colored dress shirts, and silver platform shoes. The band members wore dark blue jumpsuits to match our shirts. Our costumes were chosen specifically for our routine. They complimented our dance moves and added just enough pizzazz to get the crowd roaring. Our pants zipped at the bottom from mid-calf to ankle. After a specific dance sequence we would remove our jackets and unzip our kick pleats, showcasing a considerable amount of extra material and revealing the silver, red, and blue that matched our jumpsuits, giving us the dramatic effect we needed. We used this in our high leg-kick sequence, enhancing the flare of the pant and adding a flash of fiery intensity. Man, we looked good.

Our routine began with our backs to the audience. The song "Bad Luck" by Harold Melvin and the Blue Notes began. On the eighth count, we would start dancing and singing, and after a few verses we would break into a music bridge, take off our jackets, unzip the pleats and showcase our routine. The burst of color and choreography were the ignition to the audience's ravenous roar of approval. The crowd exploded with energy and everyone's intensity turned around. They applauded and screamed for more, and we gave it to them. When we delivered, they cheered us on as if the underdog had turned it around in the final seconds of a boxing match. We felt alive and accepted, and of course, we felt we had arrived. With struts and backwards twirls, we concluded our first song of the second set. The crowd was responding great to every song we played.

The last song "The Love I Lost," by the Spinners, was where I got the microphone and started arousing the crowd's ego. With instrumental music behind me, I began a rhythmic dialogue between the crowd and myself, the kind professionals use on stage. "How you feeling tonight?" I yelled. They replied with a roar of excitement. "Party, Party, ooh ah- ooh ooh ah, all the ladies, Miss Sadie's in the house say oaaw. All the fellows say hoo," I hollered over the microphone.

I approached a few people in the crowd and gave them the spotlight. They would sing the words to a familiar song, and the audience loved it. The ladies squirmed with anticipation, swarming Greg and me when they could. My aim with the ladies was to appeal to the jollier girls in the bunch or the elderly women of the crowd, while Greg's ego took him to the attractive females. Even still, it was tactical and calculating, the way we operated. Every move was well thought out in advance and only when the opportunity lent itself, did we improvise. While massaging the audience's need for more, I immediately darted for the fellow who called me out in the beginning of the night. I approached him with the mike, and with the spotlight on him, called him up on stage and had him participate in a few exciting chants to the ladies. He felt like a star. He ate it up and everyone loved it.

Greg and I broke out into our individual dance routines, and I rushed the dance floor. I performed some local moves for the ladies and they performed for me. They were gyrating and slithering their bodies on top of one another and vying for my attention at whatever the cost. I was headed back towards the stage when all of a sudden the black man who'd previously embarrassed me took the microphone and yelled out, "Give it up, this boy be gray." I nearly cried in that moment, as the raw feeling of acceptance came over me. My band members looked at me and nodded with approval. Everyone cheered. I learned a lesson that night and realized I now had a grasp, an inkling of what my brothers faced every day. That night we were one.

THE SEED

The result of the crowd and I becoming one was the seed for my future in wanting to bring people together. I had learned so much about racism that night through my personal experience. It opened the door to my acceptance of differences among people. It showed me we're all different but all the same. It gave me the ability to be a better crowd host. I let walls down, which enabled me to approach people in my show that I might otherwise be cautious about. It allowed me to see that there is always a way; I just need to find the appropriate angle to take.

Later that night, the celebration went to my house. The typical routine to closing up a night was to end it with a party full of drugs and alcohol. We had marijuana, an assortment of pills, cocaine, and a bar full of booze. Life was happening. I had the music, the money, my family, and all the attention and approval I needed from the crowd. And now I had drugs, the last of my necessities needed to carry out the night. Everything was good. However, that night something clicked. I realized the band and I had what it took to make it in the business, to be on the top of the charts. It was the one other thing I didn't have, the thing I longed for: success on a major level.

The band had always been on common ground together, after the same goal: success. But unfortunately, after some time, things changed. The fire went out; the hunger to make it seeped from their souls. They were content with what they had. I was blissfully unaware of this till a series of occurrences woke me up. Slowly I began to realize we were going nowhere, and unless we were to do something more with the group, it was time for me to exit. Gail had issues with my heavily booked-up schedule and wanted more family time. Unless the band made it big, she felt it was my time to go, even threatening to leave me if I stayed with the band. There were many occasions where we were presented the opportunity to move forward and make a name for ourselves. No one was willing to take the risk but me.

On one particular occasion, a couple of local booking agents, one from North Providence and one from Fall River, offered us a record deal. They'd seen our show many times. They often visited the clubs we played, as we were one of the more popular bands on the scene in those days. However, they seemed a bit shady; kind of like wise guys, so to speak, but nevertheless we were being offered a record contract. Included in the deal was a guaranteed record album and a professional band road tour throughout the country in exchange for an 80/20 split. All we needed to do was show up and the rest would be taken care of. In my eyes, it was a deal of a lifetime. While twenty percent isn't a big piece of the pie, in the long run, we had a big future ahead of us. We would be exposed to thousands of fans for a chance at making it big. We would get a chance to get deep in the business and perhaps find ourselves on the radio someday.

The guys in the band didn't feel the same. They felt the split was unfair and didn't think the record agents were trustworthy. My continued plea to them was that twenty percent of something was better than one hundred percent of nothing. "This is our chance, our time," I repeated over and over. But the guys wouldn't budge, and I gave up trying to persuade them.

Not long after, we found ourselves in the midst of another interesting opportunity to get major television publicity. It was the late-70s, and the state was in an uproar over the hunger strike that began at the local ACI (Adult Correctional Institute) in Cranston. The news coverage extended worldwide as leading news stations covered the story and newspapers were flooded with headlines of the chaos for weeks. I saw this situation as an opportunity to cash in on free local publicity and maybe even national publicity as well. I knew the sports/health official over at the prison, a guy named Chubby Gomes, whom I'd grown up with from the Point. I pitched him the idea of getting the band into the prison to play a free concert in hopes of diffusing the rioting caused by the strike. He agreed this was a great idea and would firm things up with his superiors. I made a few other calls, one to a local politician to get a feel for his opinion. He thought my idea might in fact be the answer to the ending of this strike. He was very excited and asked if he might help in getting this accomplished. I was raring to go, filled with much excitement and anticipation. I contacted two local news stations and they too were game for the idea, agreeing to give us the top story in the evening news.

I called the guys to my home for an emergency meeting, where I pitched the entire story to them, soup to nuts. Like a blunt object to the head, they shocked the life out of me when they all agreed that this was a bad idea. "Too risky," they said. "It wouldn't be safe."

After some time discussing and once again pleading my case, the decision was no. I realized if I wanted to do anything, it would have to be on my own. I felt the band had changed direction and was no longer moving forward. They seemed to be only interested in a sure thing and, well, in this industry, nothing is certain. It was time to make a new mark, and so I left the band. It was a hard hit to my heart. These guys were my family. I felt like I'd lost a limb. I was heartbroken to no longer have them or any aspect of the band life to go back to. A big part of my identity was on that stage: a crowd-pleaser, a stage performer, a lead front-man, and a man with a conviction to passionately commit to the audience. It was quite the job detaching myself from the heartbreak.

My day job over at Narragansett Business Forms helped to fill in the gaps. I had been employed with the business for about three years, and the stability of another income helped cushion the blow of having left the band. Meanwhile, I had been introduced to a co-worker by the name of Ronnie Grennier. He was a disc jockey who played "oldies parties" and kids' school dances. Some of his music repertoire consisted of The Skyliners, The Duprees, Dion, Elvis, Bill Haley and The Comets, The Hully Gully, and The Twist. As for the kids' school dances, he played Aerosmith, Bruce Springsteen, Kiss, Def Leopard, Commodores, Michael Jackson, Rick James, and some others. I was intrigued by his line of work and wanted to know more. I asked to borrow his collection to get a feel for the music. He agreed and lent me his records, separating them by genre and tempo. I sifted through the songs to determine the good and more popular from the bad and not listened to, all the while developing a notion of how this might work in a career for me. I spent several evenings making cassettes and copies of the songs. I would often dance to a tune to feel its energy and likeability. Is it a crowd-pleaser? Would the ladies like it? Would it stop a crowd in its tracks? Ronnie continued to help, giving me the ins and outs of each group and artist. I avidly listened and wrote down everything he said. A lot of the input he gave was about bands that were way before my time. Information about them was like gold. Knowing the history of artists and their mark on the music industry was one of the keys to any show I would put together. I figured I would be another oldies DJ or maybe a club DJ, and I thought the kids' shows might also work.

Taking some of the new music and insight I had, I planned a huge birthday party for my wife at the Brightridge Club in East Providence. This night was going to be a very important night, with a guest list a mile long. It would include everyone special to me, as well as a few of the band members and the two booking agents who'd offered the band the record deal. My aim was just to have a great time. I went from store to store and purchased a huge assortment of music to continue to add to my integrated music show. My selections were derived from my family's preferences. Each and every one of them had a vastly different taste in music. My sister Florence preferred oldies. So I purchased oldies records and included everything from slow easy tempos to fast upbeat ones that she liked personally. I had learned from my earlier years with the band that varying the tempo is critical when playing to a crowd. People need an assortment of moods to choose from.

The next records purchased were Billy Joel's "Glass House" and Credence Clearwater's "Proud Mary." These were my brother Alton's picks. Phyllis, my sister, loved Cream's "White Room" and Janice Joplin's "Piece of My Heart." My parents loved Andy Williams' "Moon River," The Chordettes, and "Mr. Sandman," and Mom especially loved Nat King Cole's "Ramblin Rose." A few others my dad liked were Glen Miller, Tommy Dorsey, and Duke Ellington's "Satin Doll." "The big band sound is back in town" was my scripted introduction. The extended family's picks were The Olympics' "Hully Gully," Peggy Lee's "The

Alley Cat," and lastly, The Hokey Pokey. The music I contributed was disco and funk; a collection I had from the band, and some Motown. Not too many bands could do a good job with the Motown sound. The big songs of the time were "Jeremiah was a Bullfrog," "Mustang Sally," and "Proud Mary," to name a few.

With the music in place, I retreated to my basement night after night to work on the DJ set. I had a PA system comprised of two speakers; an amplifier to increase the sound; a mixer, which allows variation in sound levels; a microphone; and a vocal zapper, which is a small apparatus used to precisely reduce vocals from a record or cassette player. With the use of my equipment, I choreographed each and every moment of the birthday party. I rehearsed my routine, wrote the lines to my Vegas-style introduction. I compiled my music into specific stylized categories, strategically coupling songs that seemed unfit together, labeling songs "showstoppers/fire songs," indicating their ability to spark the fire of dance in everyone's core. I was identifying and labeling timeless love songs used to attract couples of all ages to the dance floor and worked on my rap performance, which utilized the ability of the vocal zapper. In these days karaoke wasn't heard of, and removing vocals from a track was something only the professionals did in the studio. I knew I would definitely blow the minds of everyone invited. I would be showcasing the emergence of disc jockeying in a way never seen before--displaying the art of emceeing, rapping, and performing, while simultaneously merging various forms of music. This, coupled with a club-like experience, would be revolutionary, a new way of partying.

Ready to conquer my first show, I needed a practice arena to perform for. I had heard my former band was playing a local show in Cranston at the Sunburst Lounge. I headed there with my stage costume attire, dressed to kill. Tonight would be pivotal in determining the success of my show. I approached the guys for permission to perform during their intermission. Instead of a prerecorded cassette tape playing for the crowd, I would perform my version of "Rappers Delight" by the Sugar Hill Gang, the first popular rap song to hit America.

With the instrumental version of the song beginning, I took to the stage. "Everybody clap your hands" I yelled. I nodded to the beat and narrated a journey I took to New York City, a story I made up for entertainment purposes. I told them of meeting a group of guys who were doing something different-- instead of singing to a song, they were talking, rapping to the music, while being directed by the famous Mr. Smokey Robinson. That caught everyone's attention. People's eyes widened; some paused in the midst of heated conversations. My former band members stared. Everyone noticed. That's when I began my version of the rap. Most of the lyrics were the originals, but some of it was customized to Rhode Island and my personal endeavors, which sparked the crowd's energy even more. They went crazy, wild about the song. They yelled and applauded, even chanted various parts with me. The crowd was responding great. With a full dance floor, the groove was intense. The horn player from the band looked at me with a warm smile and said, "You're something else." From that moment on, I knew I was onto something. This energy was what I needed to shut down the negative voices inside me. The drive from that night gave me a confidence I needed for the events that were about to unfold.

The night of Gail's birthday party finally came. Everyone arrived as expected and mingled for a bit in the hall. A selection of popular slow dance songs started a great tempo. People danced, mingled, and were responding to just about everything I played. Once the dance floor was full, I would change to a different style of music, mainly to accommodate the guests that were sitting down, making sure everyone was having a good time. After about two hours or so I directed the guests to their seats and announced the show was about to begin.

THE SILENT CHANGE

Backstage, I changed into my outfit. It was show time. I had an anxious feeling of fear in the pit of my stomach, one that fellow entertainers said was a sign of professionalism. The feeling was intense, and still to this day, I feel it at the beginning of every show. With a prerecorded introduction, an announcement came over the speaker introducing my new stage name derived from the band scene. "One of New England's finest, please put your hands together for Junior Ray." The crowd responded, cheering and clapping. I threw open the curtain and took my entrance on stage. Dressed in a satin white lapelled suit, with a long rear coattail and shining red rhinestones and a black vampire cape, I began my dance number to the song "Bad Luck" by Harold Melvin and The Blue Notes. It was a song I had performed many times before while in the band. The crowd loved it.

I then took the microphone and, with the instrumental version of "Three Times a Lady" by Lionel Richie playing, I began to serenade my wife by singing to her our favorite love song. As tears ran down her face, I looked her in the eyes and kissed her lips. This brought other couples' hearts closer and I could tell the crowd was feeling tender. I then brought my wife to the dance floor and continued our romance by playing another love song and inviting all lovers to join us. Once the couples were together, my opportunity became clear. I took this chance to play the much controversial mixing of music to my guests in a highly anticipated moment of reaction. Fading out the music of Lionel Richie, I turned up the volume to "Ladies Night" by Kool and the Gang. The party was finally here and was a stunning success. The compliments were endless and the crowd was buzzing with approval. I was high on something new, something different. I had arrived. This was the moment that would change everything. That evening one of the booking agents, approached me saying, "You're onto something here." With that, I sprang forward, putting every last bit of energy and sweat into this new emerging business known as disc jockeying.

I needed to spread the word about my discoveries to the local DJs of the area. I wanted to let them know of my success. Their responses were an unfortunate ringing in my ears, negatively cutting into my excitement. They thought it was impossible to mix music of different genres at one function. They claimed my experience with the birthday party was a fluke and that people would simply not accept this kind of thing. But I was determined to continue with my plans to play weddings and functions of all sorts, mixing music and entertainment, emceeing as well as being a DJ. They just laughed at me. They said people would never accept records at their wedding; it was classless, cheap, and degrading. I would prove them wrong and would stop at nothing until I did.

TURNING A CORNER

The year was 1979. In transition, I had a tall order to fill. The goal was to achieve and maintain a salary in the music industry. I needed to make a living doing something. Local entertainers said it wouldn't work. "You can't mix oldies with rock, black music with country music, and the Hully-Gully with the 4.4 disco sound. It would be an absolute turn off. Egos were on fire. The more they said it couldn't be done, the more I said it could. "You can't," "I can." "You won't!" "I will." And with that, I set out to prove my theory. I thought more, I imagined more. I knew people wanted to mingle; they wanted to let their hair down. And so, I set out on a mission.

I approached three or four local wedding bands, asking them to hear out my idea of the integrated music show, one which combined an array of musical genres and beats through the spinning of records by a disc jockey. They replied with snubs, sneers, and fretted looks of disdain, only to answer me with "Never." They thought it would be low-grade and cheap, and people would never allow it or accept it. Record playing, alone? You'd have to be a fool. "You have to be live to be paid," they said. I remembered the parties I played at friends' homes and mine and thought to myself, "I'm live." I remembered the boring music I had at my own wedding and thought, "It's time to show them what a real party can be like: excitement, fun, and style." I would be an excellent crowd host. I recalled a time when I had vacationed in Bermuda and heard a man who introduced the band by saying, "Ladies and Gentlemen, welcome tonight. Leave your cares behind and have a good time." I remember feeling alive because of this, and I felt the presence of something special that stayed with me the whole night. They had set the stage for me that night. And every show I did, I too, always set the stage. I realized people desperately needed this. People wanted to, but actually didn't know how to party in a group. I was determined to show them how, and I did it every show. From the first song to the last, I would work on sending them back into the "normal world" with a new outlook on people, music, and life.

Live bands disapproved of my ideas, too, because DJs would be their competition. I regarded their opinion as typical, knowing that anyone in their shoes would have this uncomfortable fear of the unknown. This was unfamiliar to people. Of course, I would get negative feedback; doing things against the grain is awkward and unusual. I now knew I needed to move forward on gut instinct alone. I knew this path was important, a destiny waiting to be uncovered.

THE SHOW

I began to market my show by word of mouth, playing gigs for next to nothing. I began with benefits, which led to Christmas parties, which led to birthday parties, which eventually brought me to the huge money maker: weddings. However, when I finally booked a gig for a wedding, it was always coupled with a band, and I would get very little playtime.

My big break came when I got a gig to play a local restaurant/banquet facility in Harrisville, RI. It would prove to be a crucial moment in the DJ industry. The banquet hall was one of the more popular banquet halls in the area, Wright's Farm Restaurant. I had gotten my foot in the door when I played a softball benefit there, and after several gigs, my services became highly recommended to any interested parties who walked through their door. The owner, Mr. Frank Galleshaw, would sit in on my shows and observe me.

THE SILENT CHANGE

One night Mr. Galleshaw approached me and asked if I would play for a Christmas party he was putting together for his staff and family. I would be an added musical element to the main attraction — a prestigious eighteen-piece orchestra from Connecticut. I would perform my show during the three intermissions the band took, lasting twenty minutes each.

I immediately got to work to prepare for the big night. I had purchased extra equipment to accommodate the enormous room, worked on my vocal emceeing, and regrouped my music library. The night of the show arrived and I was raring to go. With everything in place and set up, I moved to the rear of the hall to get a reading on the crowd. There was a good mix of people, and a large age range. Wright's Farm employed at least a hundred people, and with the addition of family and friends, the Christmas party totaled a whopping three hundred people.

THE SILENT CHANGE

The band started their set. They looked impressive and professional. They were comprised of a rhythm section made up of a guitar, bass, keyboards, and drums coupled with a full string ensemble complete with violins, and of course, a brass section of trumpets, trombones, and saxophones, both alto and tenor.

The energy in the air was relaxed, with people swaying to "Moonlight Serenade" by Glenn Miller. There was an assortment of big band songs, including the waltz, the fox trot, and an entertaining medley of Frank Sinatra songs. The band was great. A few older couples got up to dance, and they really put on a show when "Chattanooga Choo Choo," also by Glen Miller, was played. When the song ended, the band took their break. That was my cue. I took the mike and started the evening with a quote my dad gave me, "Never wait for someone else to start your party, 'cause you might wait all night." Madonna's "Holiday" into "Brick House" by The Commodores pumped through the speakers and everyone's pulse came to life. The dance floor, full to capacity, shook with a thunderous vibration. Young and old danced, and people began their chants as I called them to the floor by name. I always made a point of knowing the key people to bring into the show. The audience would whistle and yell with delight when a familiar name was called. I called Frank Galleshaw up and everyone went wild.

The aisles in between the tables were full to the brim with people entranced in the moment. The twenty-minute break extended to thirty-five minutes and the crowd couldn't get enough. My set ended and the band came back to the stage. They grabbed the attention of people whose musical interest was jazzy and instrumental. That made up about a tenth of the crowd. While they played, I had a small gathering of excited people in front of my DJ table requesting songs and asking questions. At one point, I was so bombarded, I had to leave the area for the crowd to disperse. The band once again had some ballroom dancers, but the atmosphere had changed. The crowd's interest in what I had to play kept a revolving group of people coming back and forth to my turntables. The band's set was just about ending when I gathered up my heavy-hitting songs: Bruce Springsteen's "Dancing in the Dark," KC and the Sunshine Band's "Get Down Tonight," and Average White Band's "Pick up the Pieces." When I played the first song, the crowd exploded with energy, rushing the dance floor. They were caught up in the musical excitement. When the last of the three songs ended, I faded in solid gold's memory lane for the older crowd, playing The Skyliners and a little bit of Elvis. Even while playing '50s music, there was no age gap. Everyone who'd been on the dance floor previously was now enjoying the sounds of the classics. It was yet another example of people accepting musical values of all kinds.

With the crowd in hand and everyone thirsting for more, I faded out Elvis, only to kick up the notch with the '50s rock 'n' roll sounds of Dion, Elvis, and

THE SILENT CHANGE

Chuck Berry's "The Twist." It was a collaborative track, combining all three songs exploding into one another. I told the crowd that it all started back in 1955, they called it rock 'n' roll, and since then the world hasn't been the same. People lost it! They shook, they shimmied, they twisted, they roared with happiness. The little children mimicked their parents, twisting and falling, couples twisted and dipped each other, and older folks showed off their true authentic dance moves while others admired them.

I took the mike and asked the audience to clap to the beat as I faded into an instrumental version of Sugar Hills' "Rappers Delight." The crowd was glowing with excitement. They swayed and clapped while I performed my version of the rap song, using little nuances to highlight Frank and his crew. They ate it up. I continued to personalize the song, improvising important names and dates attached to this occasion. I added humor and wit, ingredients that added more excitement to the night. I pointed out the chefs, the wait staff, and the maître d' as well as the owner and his family. They were all now absolutely sold on my show and caught up in the mood of the night. No one was sitting; everyone, and I mean everyone, in that room was dancing. The orchestra's break of twenty minutes had turned into an hour. Growing impatient, they returned to the stage. They asked me to fade out the song that was playing, Michael Jackson's "Wanna Be Starting Something," and they would fade in the same song using their instruments. This orchestra was that good--they could line up note-for-note with the exact spot the song was at.

As the band began their set, the crowd cleared the dance floor. They weren't buying anything the band produced, and the only remaining couples there were ballroom dancers. Frank and his wife had a moment together waltzing, which grabbed the audience's attention for a brief time, but after that the room was sullen. Here Frank had a highly paid, talented orchestra, that didn't give or produce nearly the excitement and high-energy fun my show did. He looked around at the mood of the crowd and made the groundbreaking decision of a lifetime, a decision that would affect the DJ industry for all time. He decided to have a DJ only, host the rest of the night and relieve a $6,000-dollar-a-night orchestra of their last set, allowing them to go home early. He asked me, "Junior, do you think you could handle the rest of the evening?" The chills filled my body, I was teary-eyed and emotional. I lit on fire with excitement and hit the crowd with both barrels. The night exploded. This was another turning point in the business. I felt so proud to be a part of this journey. I took the mike and asked the audience to give a warm hand to the band, mentioning their names, their skill, their instruments, and the honor it was to accompany such a quality act. The crowd was back, intense as ever, and ready to go.

Frank had the employees move the tables to the rear of the room, providing more dance floor area. The party was a stunning success, and no one wanted the night to end. He hired me for two additional hours and from then on, I became Frank's personal entertainer and main attraction. I was the featured DJ on their formal written wedding packages, I disc-jockeyed all the family weddings, and I was gaining momentous popularity through word of mouth.

Another big night marking the validity and success of my show occurred at the Venus De Milo, a large banquet facility in Swansea, Massachusetts. People in those times were still a bit leery of the DJ show. Questions lingered as to whether hiring a band or a DJ was more appropriate for weddings. However, the show I was booked for involved two friends of mine, Eddie and Alicia Aroujo who had just gotten married and knew my show was worth booking. Although we were friends, to make sure the family and friends had every amenity available to them, Eddy and Alicia hired a seven piece band, known as Elite, in addition to my show to play their reception. The evening was held in the grand ballroom known as the

Athena III. The Venus, another ballroom, also accommodated three other functions simultaneous to Eddy and Alicia's reception, all of which were weddings.

The live band began their set. Comprised of a female lead singer, two horn players and a four man rhythm section, they began their show with soft easy Motown music. At precisely seven o' clock sharp, they announced the introductions for the wedding party. Once the bride and groom were seated, the crowd sat down for dinner and the band took their break. I then began my show. Following suit with some easy classic songs, I began my show. As they dined, I performed my rendition of soft and easy dinner music. The music selection that accompanied my narration was Nat King Cole's "Unforgettable" and Tony Bennett's "I Left My Heart in San Francisco." I then picked up the tempo slightly and played the Drifters' "Up On The Roof" and the Temptations' "Since I Lost My Baby." Alternating from slow to light tempo, I then went back to easy listening and played Johnny Miller's "Misty" and Lionel Richie's "Three Times A Lady," always zeroing in on the stars of the show, the Bride and Groom. I would also keep a watchful eye on the co-stars of the show, the crowd. It was my job to tailor the night to the bride and groom but also to read the guests and to know what they needed before they did. I was an entertainer, and my job was to give each one of them the best night of their life, and that meant everyone in that room. As my set came to end, I exited, singing a few dinner numbers, knowing live vocals would be a feature they hadn't really seen from a DJ. The band then began their second set. They played a standard mixture of ballads and a few up-to-date dance numbers as well as the bride/groom dance, the traditional wedding festivities such as the bouquet and garter toss and the parents' dances. Once the festivities ended, the band finished their set with a dance number attracting around 25 or so people to the dance floor. I, in the meantime, had been asked not to play certain songs that the band was scheduled to play so not to steal any thunder from the band. But that would soon prove to be an uncontrollable happening. When I then began my second set following the band, I played a current popular song by Aretha Franklin, "Jump To It". The introduction of the song rang out to the bar area. I remember Eddy and Alicia hurrying back in excitement to join the dance floor with many guests following behind them. The dance floor began to fill. I played three top dance songs back to back, narrating the excitement with my mic. "Everybody say pahhhhrtaay!!" The crowd responded, "partayy". I repeated myself, "Everybody say pahhhrtayy!!" They replied a second time even louder, "partaay". "All the ladies in the house say "Owww". "Oww" "All the fellows in the house say "Ooh ahh Ooh ooh aah". They responded, "ooh ahh ooh ooh aah". The whole dance floor followed suit. Excited, I climbed up on top of the bass speaker and finished my chanting. People screamed in approval. The dance floor filled to

111

capacity and people danced wherever they could find room. The night was panning out to be very similar to the Wrights Farm show I played for Frank Galleshaw with the effects of the band and the response of the crowd behaving almost identically to one another. On and on I went with the chanting. The crowd ate it up. "Shit- god damn- get off your ass and jam". They repeated me. They loved it. Suddenly a band member approached me and asked me to calm it down so they could reenter the show with their next set of music. The band started their set with a popular dance tune and the crowd dissipated to a few people. Guests in anticipation of my next set, approached me making requests for more songs, only this time they were requesting all the same songs the band played. I was trying all night to do what was asked of me and avoid playing any songs the band played. It was becoming increasingly more difficult as the night played out. The band played the last song of their set, and I began mine. I announced loudly to the crowd, "Hey people, are you ready"? The crowd responded with a series of "yeahs" and approval. I cranked the music and upon the first song, the dance floor got packed again and everyone was fired up. At that moment, I knew I had to give the crowd what they wanted. Inevitably, I played an entire list of songs, back to back, all of which were popular hits and many of which were, in fact on the bands song list. My hands were tied. I had to give the crowd what they wanted. The crowd roared and glowed with energy. Eddy and Alicia's reception was incredible.

The crowd had a great time, and it was just as intense and exciting as the Wright's Farm show, almost identical. As the energy got bigger and bigger, I noticed a crowd gathering at the entrance of the ballroom. To my shock, it included guests from the other weddings as well as their band members. What was happening here? People standing at the doorway were overwhelmed with the kind of show I put on. They hadn't ever seen or been part of anything like

113

that before, and their entertainment couldn't compete with what I was doing.

Shortly after this, the bride and groom from one of the other ballrooms came into our wedding reception and introduced themselves to Eddy and Alicia. They asked if it would be all right if they and their bridal party joined our party for a bit. They spent the rest of the night moving in and out of their room to hang in ours. It was clear this was where the party was at. I absolutely couldn't believe my eyes. This was astounding! And, as if it couldn't get any bigger or better than that, moments later another bride and groom from a different wedding appeared, asking if they too could join our reception. What a compliment. I felt ready to explode with happiness and joy. I don't think a better compliment exists than what I experienced that night. That was off the charts.

The rest of the night was an explosion of dynamics; show-stopping energy filled the air. To this day, Eddy and Alicia still speak of the amazing night they had. They believe that their wedding was hands down the absolute best party they've ever had or witnessed, and claim that their guests agree with them. Eddy and Alicia, you are two of the best people I know. I love you both.

Another powerful quality my DJ show had was that it brought people together from all walks of life. An example of this was a wedding located in Pawtucket, RI at a place called the LeFoyer Banquet Facility. It was an Italian wedding with over 250 guests, all close family and friends of the bride and groom. As I mingled with the crowd, I could feel a dampening stress overshadowing the bride and groom's big day. The father of the bride soon let me in on what the problem was. Apparently, his three brothers were feuding and hadn't spoken or seen each other for fifteen years. They were all in the room now, and much tension filled the air. The father said to me, "Ray, I am the only one who speaks to everybody. My brothers are strong in their convictions and each one of them thinks the others are wrong. Please tread very carefully when handling the evening. At any moment things could blow up." My thoughts ran a mile a minute. This feud could be the spotlight of the show if I handled it properly.

I'd planned an Italian theme, and started the night with some favorites like Dean Martin's "That's Amore," and Lou Monte's "Pepino, the Italian Mouse." Then I began serenading them from table to table, performing songs by Nat King Cole, Tony Bennett, and of course Frank Sinatra. I would take the instrumental and sing to it, allowing audience participation during the chorus lines in the song. Usually, I would sing a line then allow them to sing the next word in the coming line, and so forth and so on. I would personalize the songs to certain tables and dedicate songs to other tables. Each and every time I did something, I made certain to direct my attention to a table that had one of the brothers at it. I felt this was slowly chipping away at some of the tension and hopefully relaxing them a bit.

While I subtlety focused my attentions on the brothers, I continued to keep my energies on the bride and groom. We did toasts, cake-cutting ceremonies, and the works. Acting like I didn't know anything about the brothers' feud, I constantly mentioned how important family is and how important togetherness is. My comments were planting seeds, and to this day, I still remember the importance and power of that warm family feeling. The chipping-away experience and the miracle that ends this story is what keeps me going.

Everyone was feeling great. It was now time for the routine I had worked out in my head, hoping to bring this family together, at the very least, in a photograph or picture of some sort. What ensued was much more than I bargained for. A miracle happened before my eyes, and everyone in that room was floored with the outcome. To this day, I'm beside myself with having witnessed what came next.

With mike in hand, I asked for everybody's attention on the dance floor. I had the bride and groom seated in chairs and instructed the bride to call certain people to come forward. She asked me what I was doing, and I quietly asked her to go along with me and to trust me. I told the crowd the bride had a special presentation and she and her new groom would require the assistance of some very special family members. The bride took the mike and did as I asked. My plan was to bring all four brothers to the dance floor one at a time. This was a delicate task and needed to be handled with precision for a successful outcome. I directed her to invite brother number one to the dance floor, and asked him to stand near the already existing people in line. I then asked the bride to gather someone from each table, to add six more people to the line. I then brought up brother number two and had him join the line. With this continuing, I had the groom call up a few special people to the line, having him include brother number three. Lastly, I called the father of the bride — brother number four — and his wife to the floor. With about twenty guests on stage, including all four brothers, I pointed the audience's attention to the bride and groom. I said they had been entertaining the crowd all evening and giving the most of themselves, and that they were a great leading man and lady. They had been entertaining their family and friends and now it was their turn to relax and be entertained with a song and dance. The crowd roared with agreement. I then looked to the line of family and friends and back to my assistant at the DJ table and said "Music maestro, please."

"Start spreading the news…" "New York New York" by Frank Sinatra began. Everyone applauded with delight. "A chorus line isn't anything without a strong crowd; do I have a strong crowd?" I yelled. Again, the energy was on fire, and the crowd responded with excitement and power. I directed the line of people, now known as my chorus line, to sway

119

from side to side in harmony with the song. As the first line was sung, I walked up the line of people until I got to the first brother, and leaned the mike into him to finish the line out. I continued doing this with random people and then leaned the mike to brother number two, a few more guests, then brother number three. When the song got to the bridge of the song, "It's up to you, New York, New York," I instructed the chorus line to do the high leg-kick sequence we associate with the Rockettes. With the audience going crazy I then went to brother number four, the father of the bride, pointed out his leg-kicking skills, and asked him to sing the last bits of the song. At the end of the song I yelled, "How about a warm round of applause for one hell of a chorus line?" I had the chorus line bow and take their moment in the spotlight. I then welcomed them to the world of show business. I told them the father of the bride had invested a large amount of money into a few blank recording contracts, and if anyone in the chorus line wanted to change their profession, they needed to take part in a second audition. They did, however, need to read the fine print which stated "Don't call us, we'll call you."

By this time, everyone was in hysterics and feeling so good. All of a sudden, one brother walked to another brother with a look of forgiveness and love. He grabbed him and hugged him for a moment, then gestured for the other two brothers to join them. In the center of the dance floor, the four brothers hugged and wept. This was an incredible moment, to say the least. It was a defining moment in my DJ carrier, another validation of my goals. This show was magical in every sense of the word. Many in the room hugged each other and wept. The father of the bride thanked me with a big hug and said, "This was one of the most amazing moments in my life, and we owe you our gratitude. Thank You." The whole family cried tears of joy. Everyone was hugging and kissing, and this went on all night. Almost everyone in the room at one time or another thanked me for bringing the family together and said the show was outstanding. I left there feeling on top of the world. I realized my faith in the power of music had grown to immeasurable heights that night. Never had it been so solidified and strong. That night was a testament to the miracles that occur in our lives. What took place was bigger than all of us that day. Something great had happened. The silent change occurred and was responsible for all of this. It was then I realized my path had been set. It was unknown to me at the time, but when I look back I can see it clearly.

I had an epiphany that night. I learned that people are all good, but many are burdened with fear, a terrible crippling emotion that places them in an uncomfortable place, causing anger, resentment, hate, gossip, and jealousy. These emotions, being so raw and uncomfortable, show their face without regard to the setting. In my show, however, with the help and evolution of the silent change, we only sell love, happiness, and a great time with good memories.

122

Togetherness is the backbone of what I do, of what I 'm trying to produce in every setting and every show. We all want to have a good time, in spite of ourselves. My job has become responsible for breaking down those walls of fear and giving people the night of their lives, "dancing till dawn"!

THE SHOW MUST GO ON

I lived to make people feel good. I never felt good unless the audience felt good. That was my weakness and my strength. On one hand, my desire reflected the people-pleaser in me, running for everyone and putting their needs first. On the other hand, people-pleasing catapulted my success in the entertainment industry. The formula for my show was making sure everyone in the crowd felt good. My job became the focus of every pursuit in my life's goal. I made certain everyone felt a part of something-- something big--the crux of life. Celebrating life with music and dance in the company of loved ones is at the heart of life's happiness. This jewel, the gem of life, was a formula I had a gut feeling about. Many times people need to have the party started for them. People needed an instruction to get up and dance, to have fun. Once that truth became clear to me, I ran with it. I asked questions like, how can I fix everyone? How can I make everyone smile? I needed to create a show with music and energy that would appeal to everyone.

The ever so familiar cliché, "You can't please everybody" was said over and over again and again to me. What could I do to please everybody? How about a show that played music for everyone? How about a show that was entertaining, a show that was clean, that didn't play loud, disrespectful music but was a respectable show that would host everyone? I knew it was possible. I didn't know the powerful impact it would have. I didn't know its potential, but with endless thoughts and ideas, the show came to life. In the beginning, I often heard "You can't do this" and "You can't do that." It was these times specifically that presented me with a challenge. My focus became "how can I make this work?" The challenges were not only exciting, they became fun.

Promoting my show was critical in the

entertainment world. It's what kept me in business for over thirty years. I used telemarketing strategies, inviting people who had previously been at my functions and reminding them of the upcoming show at a local club or venue. I usually put in a total of three calls per person. The first came one month in advance, the second followed a week before the scheduled show, and the third happened the night before or sometimes on the night of the show. In addition to that, I put out fliers on vehicles at supermarkets, flea markets, factory outlet stores, movie theaters, malls, college campuses, etc. I also did door-to-door work, informing people of the show. Lastly, I kept in touch with people by having them fill out table tent cards at private functions or local club venues. The cards read, "Let's stay in touch" and had places for the person to fill in their name, address, and telephone number. I directed the audience to fill the cards out at some point during the course of the evening. I would then perform mass mailings to every contact I had, with information on the various clubs and functions I was playing. The result was tremendous. On a Tuesday night, I could fill a club with over 500 people. The club owners loved it, and my popularity grew. Word spread about the power of the show. Many gigs were booked and to this day it continues.

I was able to see my business grow because of a few simple pointers my father gave me as I grew up. "To get respect, you must give it." "Never wait for someone else to start your party--go out and start your own." The respect quote was one of the most powerful tools in the business, I learned. It has been a very valuable philosophy, probably the most valuable. By that, I mean respect goes a long way when dealing with people. They will ultimately let their guard down and trust you once you've shown them true respect. All people want to do is to have a good time. I discovered a key to let that happen. I found out that when people are respected, they let down their walls of fear and celebrate together.

Respecting people meant playing the music of their choice, showcasing them, and dedicating the music to them. My targets were the guests of honor and the people who felt awkward. My goal was to allow them to feel special, highlighting them as the stars of my show. The rest of the crowd also had important value to me. I needed to affect every person in the room and allow them the opportunity to feel a part of something. My job was to create happiness by bringing people together through a shared musical experience.

When I host a show, part of the power of the show comes from the wide assortment of music I bring with me. This array of music is geared toward the entire crowd, having a little something for everyone. Showing the crowd respect and giving them a taste of their personal kind of music; giving a warm, friendly introduction marked with eye contact; bringing people to the spotlight; and playing music requests allows them to find themselves and drop their guard. They then will respond in a favorable way and allow themselves to have the night of their life. Without this key ingredient, respect, the show would not be a success.

I had also discovered that most people don't know how to have a good time and that the success of an evening would depend on my ability to be a good crowd host, always watching people's reactions and, most of all, paying attention to the underdog. The formula, the great formula for tremendous crowd hosting, was looking out for the ones who couldn't have a party, who couldn't have a good time. There was always a group of people who could freely express themselves and go to the dance floor following the groove of the music. But then there was the other side of the coin.

There were people who sat in their seats for the entire evening, uncertain of how to have a good time. That's where I came in. My mission for the night's success was to get the ones who wouldn't and simply couldn't enjoy themselves to the dance floor for the party of their life. I would ask myself questions like, "What can I do for them? How can I get them excited? What do they want?" The strategy I used was in the spinning of the records. I took specific, well-thought out music with altered tempos and played them at varying times to control the crowd. The end result became empty seats and a full dance floor. It was this very formula that made my show the success it was.

I would see and hear many comments and gestures from the guests indicating their approval and that they were, in fact, having a fantastic night. To add to the heightened emotion, I would often add a special request personalized and tailored to a specific individual, usually the host of the evening, but many times someone who was struggling to have a good time. When they heard the announcement over the speaker, their face would light up. Hearing a special dedication or request to the dance floor was one of the highest forms of flattery. People squirmed in their seats, delighted to be thought of.

I often did for others as I would want done for me. I thought about what it would be like to be on the dance floor with my wife and what forms of flattery would please me. What kind of behavior would I want to see from the DJ? In what way could the DJ respect me and my wife and in what ways could I be insulted? How would I as a guest want to be a part of the show? From then on, my show grew exponentially. I never dreamed it would be as big as it was. My journey was beginning.

WORD STARTED TO SPREAD

At this point, my show gained much popularity. I began noticing other disc jockeys at my gigs. They started showing up everywhere I was. I realize now they were at class — studying and observing every move I made and listening to every word I said. These were the very same DJ's that said it wouldn't work. They learned the art of mingling people together, they learned how to give respect and how to receive it, and they learned how to get people to let their hair down. It was quite a moment to witness, to see my idea come full circle to those who had opposed it. Amazing! My show was a success! So much so, I was completely booked for that year and had to turn people down. I hated doing this and purchased extra equipment to begin a second show with friends, whom I began training. I saw serious dollar signs adding up when the second show took off and I had sub-disc jockeys at the local clubs playing three nights a week. I owned three vans and three station wagons, all invested in the DJ industry. I performed two gigs a day seven days a week, and had a handful of disc jockeys underneath me running three or four gigs a week at local venues, all under the umbrella of the Jr. Ray show.

On one particular occasion, a DJ from New York, known as the Groove Master (his real name was Ronnie), came up to Rhode Island specifically to see my show. Down in New York, they hadn't heard of this music integration. He watched from the rear of the venue and afterward approached me. He said he'd never seen people react to this type of music integration and that he was surprised they were okay with it. He wondered if it would work back home. He said if people did accept it, it would open a lot of doors. He returned to one of my shows a few years later and told me he had three shows a week booked, he was making a ton of cash, and that mixed-music shows were popping up everywhere. He thanked me and went back to New York.

My show continued to grow. I played for prominent crowds, state office crowds, the Division of Motor Vehicles, and the Division of Taxation. Liquor laws weren't as strict then, and my shows would last sometimes till three or four in the morning. Local clubs celebrated for no reason at all, and partying became a norm for the locals. I thought my drug and alcohol use was totally normal. Drinking at the clubs was a given, but the drug use was a nightlife special. On one particular evening, I had been doing a show for a very prominent group of well-respected businessmen. In the men's room of the club lay a baggie filled with cocaine, a mirrored tray, and razor blades with straws. It was a community baggie for all to enjoy. When the baggie was empty, it was readily filled, and anyone who wanted the cocaine could have it for free. When we were done clubbing, more fun was to be had afterward. We'd always party in the afterhours. Tons of drugs, tons of money filled my life. It became so much so that the 305 Club shut me down.

The 305 was a local club in East Providence. It was owned by the Fraternal Order of Police, a.k.a. the FOP. It was the place to be on Thursday nights. The people coming to the club came for the hard-driving funk disco and love songs. From time to time, people came to party with drugs and alcohol. Having gone there on a number of occasions, I began to notice the power of certain songs, how they entranced people and how they became tools to direct the mood of the crowd. It was then that I really took an interest in the art and craft of music and crowd hosting. I made my visits to the club more often and eventually became their number one Disc Jockey. I partied, danced, disc jockeyed and enjoyed a comfortable relationship with the local drug dealers. I was supplied heavily and shared my drugs with many of the patrons. I was kind of like the Pied Piper; I would play the crowd and the crowd would follow. My drug use got so bad they fired me and my show. The Narcotics Squad was brought in because the level at which we were partying was completely and utterly out of control. It was bringing too much attention to the police to have that level of drugs and alcohol in and out of their club. We had to be shut down. I defended myself by pointing out the club's success on Thursday nights and how it was full to capacity. It didn't help. My employment was finished.

I admit, it did get a little out of hand, people coming up to the bandstand, shaking my hand and in the process, me slipping them a small package and receiving one in return. The drugs were out of control at the clubs--they were on the bathroom sink and on top of the toilet.

Chopping and snorting cocaine seemed harmless and normal. None of my circle of friends and relatives saw anything wrong with it. At the time we really didn't see any harm. The nightlife and drugs was our reward for a hard-working day. My daily afternoon was filled with the kids' baseball games, dance classes, Boys Club, picnics, the beach, school functions, doctors' appointments, and family outings. I tried to squeeze everything into a busy and full life so that later I could end the day with a little buzz. Little did I know, it would all come to a screeching halt all too soon.

What I didn't know was that harmless social alcohol and drug use became far more than I could handle. My life spiraled out of control. Everything that should have been happening in a normal household was not. My children's needs were neglected. Life was barely functioning. Alcohol and drugs ran my life. My every move revolved around how I would get my next supply and how much more I could ingest. The progressive disease of addiction took over.

THE CURTAIN CAME DOWN

I didn't know that I didn't know. One day in the midst of the insanity-paced drug infested lifestyle I lived, my oldest son Ray approached me and asked if I could help him with an interview he had at school. He had won the honorable principal's award at LaSalle Academy and had been contacted by the local newspaper for an interview. Without hesitation, I agreed to help. For a brief moment in time, due to very dark hours in my life, I distanced myself from the drugs and alcohol scene and planned to attend this interview sober, hoping this could be a new beginning for me. But to my disappointment, the anticipation of the interview wasn't enough motivation for me, and I began using drugs again a short time after. I was on the last day of a three-day binge when Ray approached me to remind me of the interview. I tried to refuse, and made excuses, but the dreaded look of sadness and disappointment covered my son's face, like it had, all too often. I couldn't let him down anymore. I needed to come through. I arrived at the interview feeling beat and lost. When I met the news reporter, I couldn't keep the masquerade up any longer, and I asked for his help. I told him of my condition and situation and that I couldn't bear to let my son down any more. He first interviewed Ray Jr. on his school achievement and then turned the interview to me. He pulled no punches, and I answered his questions with direct honesty and candor. I answered questions about my disgusting drug habit, how much I used, how often, about the fact that I had been awake for three days straight, and the fact that I was an addict. I also said I was a local DJ and my stage name was Jr. Ray. I agreed to attend detox and admit myself into a twelve-step program. After the interview, I returned home and called the detox center. I was then brought to the Salvation Army for a committed ninety-day treatment program.

THE SILENT CHANGE

The reporter called a few days later and said he had completed the story. He cautioned me that the nature of the information could have a negative effect on my reputation in the community and business world, but I was beat and was determined not to turn back. I said I understood and asked him to run the story. I was in the program when the article came out in the Providence Journal. I had twenty-two shows booked, and all but two were canceled once the word spread. The article read, "He wanted a story for his son. Local DJ known as Jr. Ray had his final curtain come down."

When I look back, I can see there was a seed planted that day that has grown and brought me to a place of peace and happiness I've never known.

I stayed sober for five months and then inevitably went back to drinking. My wife and I separated. I found another girlfriend to paint the town with. She drank and drugged like me. I went on a five-day-drunk escapade. I thought I had died. I sat in my van and felt like I was having a massive nervous breakdown and saw my life pass in front of my eyes. It was this moment of epiphany which brought me to my knees begging for mercy from God. I admitted myself again into the recovery program, and by the grace of God, have since been sober, twenty years to the date of this writing. I unfortunately had to quit the DJ business; the fast paced drug-infested lifestyle was undoubtedly associated with the entertainment industry. It was a place in my life that triggered many weaknesses in the disease of addiction for me and so I had to leave. A very bitter sweet decision, it was necessary for my recovery. I have also since remarried and began a new venture as the owner of a Contracting-Painting-Remodeling business where I am able to still utilize my people pleasing qualities and extroverted attributes I learned in the disc jockey business. I am also heavily involved in AA, the alcohol/narcotics recovery program where I sponsor many men and women. My hopes are remaining on the path of miracles similar to those I witnessed with the Silent Change.

After a long period of time and much life in sobriety and healing, I found I still really missed the entertainment business. I missed the people, the energy, the entertainment, the singing, and most of all the miracles. When I saw other DJs perform weddings for my families, I wanted to tell them what I knew and help improve their game. From time to time, I would do shows with my son, who had taken over my DJ business. I would continue to teach him the ropes and perform around town with an old friend, Mike McDevitt. He was a singer who sang the classics, and he and I would harmonize and sing at whatever functions we could. I realized, through the small number of times I was re-exposed to the disc jockey world with Ray and Mike that I had become physiologically strong enough to resist any temptation of drugs and alcohol. The itch for the business grew and grew and one amazing day came, and I was again reemerged into the best entertainment platform that's ever existed-Disc Jockeying. I picked up where I left off and began disc jockeying again. I reconnected with old contacts. I marketed my show to old and new clients and began to reestablish myself in the business. My son and I eventually merged our disc jockey companies together and have since created our website: www.musicshopdj.com. We are taking the New England area by storm. We have one of the best shows available and are truly a force to be reckoned with. This show is now better than ever with an added twist: "The New CELBRATE LIFE show" which brings the crowd into the power of now.

When I looked back on what I thought was a disaster and a useless life, I began to see things that amazed me. I learned more about who I was and who I wasn't. And why I was and why I wasn't. Clarity truly began to set in. What I thought was wrong was actually my way of not giving up, and continuing a path of destiny. Having defects such as people-pleasing, co-dependency, and low self-esteem, to name a few, were ways of surviving in order to live out my truth through the triumphs and pitfalls. It was necessary to embark on the path less traveled, for it was where I was meant to be and meant to go; the path that opened the door for people to come together; the miraculous-amazing path of the Silent Change. A path to bring people out of themselves to be a part of their true nature: happy, well respected, full of life and celebrating. Celebrating life and coming together like never before.

People are motivated by many forms of fear, and if left untreated, the world will be masked by a great ball of negative energy. Every pathway has a beginning, and, if left without direction, fear, self-judgment, prejudice, and low self-esteem could be the end result. These very things are the walls keeping us apart. Luckily, the power of good, the power of the Silent Change, prevailed. Now, the Silent Change no longer needs to be silent. With people coming together, it can live and grow, the same way it did in the beginning of time, when the very essence of life was first created.

It is here and now people see what they are capable of. If they drop their fear, resentment, and judgments and realize they have an immeasurable power when they act as one, life could change. We can make a difference. People have the choice — to choose to strengthen their minds, or be complacent. Should the latter occur, they could in fact be caught in a negative gravitational pull, a disease of the mind that runs rampant throughout the world. It is my job, honor and responsibility to help that change. I will not stop. I will express the true freedom of life and help affect the world of change by sharing happiness with everyone I came in contact with. We have made a difference.

The show must go on!!

Thank God, it's show time.

Junior Ray, author of *The Silent Change,* still performs in the New England area and has dedicated a big part of his life to bringing people together.

CONTACT INFORMATION

To contact Jr. Ray, The Music Shop, & my son Ray Arruda

Phone: 401-232-3851

Cell: 401-640-4349

Email: JrRayDJ@gmail.com

Website: www.musicshopdj.com

The Music Shop

A professional DJ Entertainment Company

Over 30 Years of Experience

New England's #1 Leading Entertainment Show: Our goal is to provide first-class entertainment and the perfect musical backdrop for every moment, creating an elegant atmosphere for a stunning and memorable evening. With every song perfectly planned and well thought out and having mastered all the tricks of the trade, Ray's incredible vocal ability and technique have been pivotal in providing people with a timeless and memorable evening. Maintaining the highest quality of professionalism, unparalleled service, and the utmost attention to detail, the show is equipped with an arsenal

148

of over 60,000 songs, state-of-the-art equipment, and wall and table lighting packages. With backup DJs and equipment, your function is guaranteed to be a success.

Specializing in all functions, weddings, corporate events, and family gatherings.

<u>NOTES</u>

THE SILENT CHANGE

THE SILENT CHANGE

THE SILENT CHANGE

THE SILENT CHANGE